PRAISE FOR
FROM ALLY TO ACCOMPLICE:
HOW TO LEAD AS A FIERCE ANTIRACIST

"I wasn't expecting a self-help book on racism to be a page-turner, but Seena Hodges shares profound expertise and wisdom in such an engaging and straightforward way that it's hard not to read it cover to cover. And at the end of it, the case for becoming an accomplice fighting racism is compelling, and the path forward is clear. This book will change the hearts, minds, and actions of all who read it."

David Wilson, managing partner at Commutator LLC

"It takes practice and courage to truly create and unleash the power of diversity in our lives. *From Ally to Accomplice* educates through a historical lens and empathizes with the understanding that each of us has our own set of life experiences . . . yet never lets us off the hook. Seena gives us the tools, the language, and the practical framework to elevate our awareness and confidence to make a difference."

D. Ellen Wilson, former Fortune 20 HR Executive

"Perfect for anyone who has heard themselves saying 'I don't know where to start' or 'I'm worried about getting it wrong.' The information is authentic, practical, and tangible. Transformation is possible and this book will help you understand, learn, and move to action. You can hear Seena Hodges' strong, yet kind, voice through her powerful stories and examples, which creates a safe and vulnerable foundation for the journey forward."

Amy Langer, co-founder and former owner of Salo LLC

"A must read for anyone who strives to lead, *From Ally to Accomplice* is a manual for how to really be the accomplice so many of us think we already are. The tests of leadership are never easy, and Seena Hodges challenges us all to truly reflect on what it means to stand up to racism instead of standing by."

Dave Murphy, president & CEO of Lind Electronics

"As leaders, we need to do the work to understand how to not settle for just "Diversity and Inclusion" but to actively dismantle racism in our organizations and society. *From Ally to Accomplice* is a must-read guide that contains everything you need to know if you want to lead as a fierce antiracist."

Amanda Brinkman, speaker, author, and CEO of Sunshine Studios

"Powerful, practical, and solid advice on how to approach the vast and complex topics of DEIA with confidence. Seena Hodges' expertise will change the way you think about *everything*, from day-to-day thoughts and actions to your professional life—no matter your position or industry. It's a must-read that you will find yourself going back to again and again."

Tracy Nielsen, executive director of HandsOn Twin Cities

"*From Ally to Accomplice* is nothing short of transformational. We see things differently and act differently, with an informed purpose that we didn't have before."

Maurice Blanks, co-founder and COO of Blu Dot

"We are committed to DEI work because it's the right thing to do, both personally and professionally. From a business perspective, I've always been convinced that with more diverse voices at our tables, we make better decisions and we become a stronger company—and a more dynamic and fun place to work!"

John Christakos, co-founder and CEO of Blu Dot

"*From Ally to Accomplice* is a powerful, practical read that every organization would be wise to embrace. Seena is an incredible coach with an amazing ability to be positive, even when the subject is not. She gives readers the tools and insights they need to do better, and to recognize it is incumbent on us to do so."

— **Allison Kaplan**, editor in chief of *Twin Cities Business*

FROM ALLY TO ACCOMPLICE

HOW TO LEAD AS A FIERCE ANTIRACIST

SEENA HODGES

From Ally to Accomplice© copyright 2024 by Seena Hodges. All rights reserved. No part of this book may be reproduced in any form whatsoever, by photography or xerography or by any other means, by broadcast or transmission, by translation into any kind of language, nor by recording electronically or otherwise, without permission in writing from the author, except by a reviewer, who may quote brief passages in critical articles or reviews.

ISBN 13: 978-1-63489-623-8

Library of Congress Catalog Number has been applied for.
Printed in the United States of America
First Printing: 2024
27   26   25   24   23   5   4   3   2   1

Cover design by Luke Bird
Cover photography by Desireé Wells

Wise Ink
PO Box 580195
Minneapolis, MN 55458-0195

Wise Ink is a creative publishing agency for game-changers. Wise Ink authors uplift, inspire, and inform, and their titles support building a better and more equitable world. For more information, visit wiseink.com

To order, visit www.seenahodges.com or itascabooks.com.
Reseller discounts available.

*For Willie C. Hodges, Marlene Browne,
George Lee Browne, and Emmanuel Ofori Akyea.
(Daddy, Pop-Pop, Nana, and Papa)*

TABLE OF CONTENTS

Before We Begin	11
Foreword	13
Introduction	17
Why I Do This Work	20
About Our Journey	25
On Experience and Language	30
Chapter 1: We Need Accomplices	33
PART 1: What You Need to Know to Develop Your Practice	67
Chapter 2: The Origins and Impact of Race and Racism	69
Chapter 3: White Supremacy Culture Is Always at Play	101
Chapter 4: Power and Privilege Are Your Paths to Action	119
Part 2: Creating Your Best Practice for Antiracist Leadership	133
Chapter 5: Commit to a Race-First Lens	135
Chapter 6: Acknowledge Your Racial Identity	153
Chapter 7: Define What You're Willing to Work For	167
Chapter 8: Get Curious	179
Chapter 9: Engage with Difference	201
Chapter 10: Start Taking Risks	225
Chapter 11: Your Path Forward	249
Acknowledgements	256

BEFORE WE BEGIN

A word on *Woke*

You might have noticed that my company is called The Woke Coach.

For us, woke means that you:

- Understand that each of us is only the sum of our lived experiences.

- Are aware that your own lived experience is not the quintessential lived experience--and because of this, you have to awaken to the experiences of others.

- Think about things in a racialized context. Does a specific scenario mean that race is always at play? Not necessarily, but it *could* be, and it's important to be awake to that reality.

- Do not accept situations and circumstances at face value. Consider how power, systems, and access may impact any given outcome.

Ultimately, woke means that you are paying attention to social and societal injustices and move to action to eradicate them.

This book was written in present day Saint Paul, Minnesota, on the unceded, ancestral homeland of the Dakota and Anishinaabe people past and present.

I acknowledge the forcible removal of those humans from their land through settler colonialism—that included genocide, theft, and the destruction of culture and cultural practices—among other realities. I honor and recognize the original stewards of this land and work every day to ensure that their legacy and current realities are not erased.

I urge you to find out whose land you live, work, and otherwise engage on; gain a better understanding of the specific issues of those people; and commit to continuous learning and action.

FOREWORD

"We are committed to DEIAA work because it's the right thing to do, both personally and professionally. And from a business perspective, I've always been convinced that with more diverse voices at our tables, we make better decisions and we become a stronger company—and a more dynamic and fun place to work!"
    –John Christakos, Co-founder and CEO of Blu Dot

"*From Ally to Accomplice* is nothing short of transformational. We see things differently and act differently, with an informed purpose that we didn't have before."
    –Maurice Blanks, Co-founder and COO of Blu Dot

In 2020, we hired Seena Hodges, and she completely transformed how we work and understand the world. 2020 was a year of racial awakening for many people. We were no exception. As white leaders, we found ourselves searching for ways to move forward productively and authentically after George Floyd's murder in Minneapolis, where our Blu Dot headquarters is located. The months that followed his murder were a time of confusion and self-reflection for us. "What are we doing? How did we play a role in how our city got here? Where are we within all of this, and where do we want to be?" With the shock and reflection came the honest realization that we were on the sidelines of the racial equity game. We were watching, not even playing. It's awful that such a tragedy is what it took to wake us up, but we suspect we were not unique in that way.

While it might have been a late realization, we knew we wanted Blu Dot to be in the game. We looked at where our company was headquartered and what we were doing as a company and wanted to bridge that divide. We didn't know what to do, but we knew that what we did yesterday was not what we should be doing tomorrow. George Floyd's murder changed how we felt about our company and our responsibility to the world in which our company exists.

We believed our company had the DNA to be a diverse and inclusive workplace. Collaboration and humility are among our strongest core values, and both require a lot of empathy. Our entire business model is based on everyone working together, with no one getting design credit; we had an "everybody is welcomed at our party" kind of attitude–and that felt like a great foundation for inclusion. Yet, we hadn't taken intentional and active steps toward inclusion. We posted jobs and hired whoever showed up and was qualified rather than seeking out contributors that would expand our viewpoints and, thus, our capacities. We weren't shaping our team to reflect the community around us. In 2020, we knew that no matter our foundation, our lack of awareness and intention meant our team was not as interesting or diverse as it could be.

To figure out how to actively create an inclusive environment, we started the "From Ally to Accomplice" program with our entire leadership team. It was eye-opening. Our team was made up of a spectrum of people who came to DEIAA work with different experiences and degrees of comfort around the topic of race. We were not used to talking about topics that weren't work related–our society essentially trains us not to talk about our personal lives at work. Yet, we felt such relief and connection when we finally did it.

Your team might be like ours. Maybe you're like us and not sure how comfortable you are introducing race and racial equity into a work setting and your leadership practice. We can say this: The Woke Coach's approach will work for you.

Seena has a gift for drawing connections between personal

experiences and their social implications and then enabling deep contemplation about both. She poses challenging questions we should ask ourselves daily, at home and work. Spending time answering those questions and reflecting on them has helped us grow as individual leaders and as a team. Now, our work with The Work Coach has expanded into the entire organization; not only is every employee benefiting from the experiences, but we are also all evolving together.

Our experience with Seena and her team at The Woke Coach reconstructed how we think about the world and run our multinational business. We were used to discussing traditional business questions like, "How are we going to market?" or "What's our marketing strategy?" But we were not used to asking more complex questions that shaped our leadership capabilities and business operations, like, "When did you realize you were white?" and "How does your lived experience align with or affect others when you're in a meeting?" These questions produce an entirely different line of thinking about business, leadership, and people than questions about product profitability or budgets. Yet these are questions we should ask ourselves as we prepare for business in our current and future world. We don't have the luxury of considering our product apart from the context in which it exists. The world and all the things that happen (or don't) impact our company–and all of the people working there.

The truth is, before our "From Ally to Accomplice" (re)education, we were ignorant about many things. And we were ignorant of our ignorance. We were not taught about racial identity when we were growing up. We did not learn about institutional racism or inequitable practices that resulted in inequitable outcomes. Decades into our careers, we are playing catch up, trying to learn about the deeply ingrained racial aspects of our society that shape the people we work with and people in our community. We had blind spots. Many people do.

While we are still only beginning our journey of understanding, we are grateful for what we've learned. Seena is a trusted guide who helps you constructively realize your deficiencies and opportunities and what to do about them with no shame or judgment. If you want to think critically about how you can personally and professionally grow your empathy and awareness, you've chosen the right author and book. Seena is direct and unfiltered; she challenges you with humor, joy, and warmth. This book will change how you understand your responsibility for broader social issues and how you can use that responsibility to change the world around you.

The most significant change at our organization has been how our senior leadership has shifted their mindsets. Seena always says, "Once you see injustice, you can't unsee it." That translated directly into our experience. We realized how better we could be and how much better our organization could be if we learned about injustice and actively participated in equity work. Once we realized that, we couldn't unrealize it. Nor did we want to. We want to keep going because we can always be better and get better. Seena got us to where we are now and continually inspires us to go further with our DEIAA commitments and strategies.

Read this book with your team or family, or read it alone. But read it. If you're wondering whether you should invest in moving from ally to accomplice, the answer is yes. We all have a part to play in conquering what seems like the insurmountable challenge of racism and racial inequity: collective change will only happen when everyone makes personal changes. Being a cheerleader on the sidelines is not enough. On the other side of your effort is a better you, one who is more prepared to lead in or at your company and beyond.

- John Christakos and Maurice Blanks

INTRODUCTION

I Don't Teach You How to Do Things, I Show You How to Be

I thought once we had more diversity on staff that we'd become more inclusive.
We're really struggling to retain a diverse staff.
We've tried everything. I can't believe we're not further along.
We know we're not where we need to be, but we're committed to doing the work.
We hired a director of DEI, but they already left.

Sound familiar? After years (or even decades) of work intended to improve diversity, equity, and inclusion (DEI), companies aren't making progress toward their goals. Many proclaim the desire to create more equitable and inclusive environments, but not much has changed for individuals inside of these organizations. Organizations have rushed to hire DEI leaders, and yet many of those leaders are not succeeding or staying in those roles. Copious amounts of data and first-person accounts tell us what people want and need to feel whole and included, and yet workplaces still haven't made adjustments that meet the very real needs of the people they aspire to hire and retain.

Why? Because leaders and others haven't fully committed to changing themselves and their perspectives. They haven't committed to learning and behaving in new ways that make more space for more types of people. They haven't truly engaged with the changes that need to be made, and many struggle to stay engaged and dedicated to the ongoing effort the changes will take. But there is a path forward.

Hi, friend. I am Seena Hodges, the founder of a company called The Woke Coach. I am here to give you a place to start—or deepen—your journey toward antiracist leadership. I am a connector. I am a fierce antiracist. I am an intersectional feminist. I am an equity, diversity, and inclusion champion. I am also a wife. I am a parent. I am a friend. I am an entrepreneur. I am a Black woman. I use the pronouns *she* and *her*. But above all, I love helping people succeed. It's nice to meet you.

If you've picked up this book, you probably already think of yourself as an ally: someone who supports but doesn't share the experience of a historically excluded group. Even if you don't use that label personally, you've probably also realized that allyship feels good, but it seldom leads to real change. That's because it's well-intentioned but *intermittent* support for individuals in historically excluded groups.

If you're ready to commit to making a real difference, I invite you to become an accomplice. Accompliceship is **intentional, informed continuous antiracist action for the benefit of others in which an individual believes it is their personal responsibility to risk their power and privilege in pursuit of an equitable and just society.**

Say you're Black, Indigenous, or a person of color (BIPOC), and you're sitting in a team meeting at work when Jack, a colleague, makes a racist statement (either knowingly or unknowingly). A brief silence settles on the room, and then what happens? The next few minutes unfold differently depending on whether an ally or accomplice is in the room.

An ally will hear the racist comment and immediately know that it's inappropriate. *After* the meeting, the ally will come over to you and say, "I can't believe Jack said that. He is such a jerk. I'm sorry you had to sit through that." We all suffer when inappropriate comments are shared in a common space, but the ally recognizes the harm that Jack caused with his inappropriate comment and that you, as a BIPOC, were harmed by it more than others.

The accomplice says, *immediately after the racist statement,* "Jack, that was inappropriate, whether you intended it to be or not. Can we all agree to be more careful when it comes to our use of language? There are tons of articles and other information that clearly outline what's appropriate for this context; please take the time to look them up." The accomplice's response creates a very different experience for you, as a BIPOC, and the outcomes are very different for the team and workplace as well.

The ally likely felt good because they showed up for someone who was harmed and acknowledged the unfairness of that experience. But what they really did was harm you again. Not only did you have to sit through the racist act the first time, but now you also know your colleague recognized it as such *and* didn't do anything about it *and* wants to talk to you about how terrible it was—talk about dragging out the harm! You feel worse, and yet the ally feels better because they absolved themself of the guilt of witnessing a racist action.

The accomplice, in contrast, allowed you to be seen and validated the moment it happened, so you don't have to carry shame around after the meeting. They also modeled accountability for your other, likely majority-white colleagues, which creates a culture of naming inappropriate behaviors. Another way to phrase it is creating a culture of learning, of figuring out how to be better consistently. It's important to model calling in and making a correction after making a mistake. Saying "We need to fix that language because it's hurtful to others" is not punitive if and when you've created a culture of learning and accountability. A brave space, if you will.

Such small but impactful actions illustrate the difference between an ally and an accomplice. Both demonstrate an awareness of racism, but the accomplice felt a personal responsibility to correct the issue even though the accomplice did not instigate it. And the real-time course correction not only backed up a BIPOC in the meeting but also set the entire team on a learning trajectory of doing better.

In my work, I coach people through the excuses they use for not opting in to lead as fierce accomplices. I help my clients—and now you—be the best, most understanding, empathetic versions of themselves around issues of racism, bias, inequity, and injustice. And my company name is The Woke Coach, so what does *woke* mean? What does it mean to wake up? We believe *being woke* simply means that you are paying attention to social and societal injustices. Underrepresentation and exclusion have a long history, and to change things we need everyone to wake up and challenge the status quo. How we choose to lead and who we want to be are tied directly to what we cultivate around us and how aware we are of our collective situation. I have worked with clients all over the world who want to develop an antiracist practice that prepares them to take consistent, equitable actions in their personal lives and workplaces that challenge the status quo. If you want that, too, this book is for you.

WHY I DO THIS WORK

Around 2017 I accepted a position that was my "big-time, boss-chick" moment. The opportunity paid six figures and bestowed me with a fancy title in a sector that was doing impactful work *and* had the funds to do it right. After years of working in the nonprofit sector and feeling like doing good for a living was good enough, I felt like I had finally made it! Did I mention the six-figure salary?

Then one day, about eight months into my role, the CEO pulled me aside during a work trip to San Francisco and said, "I don't think things are going as well as you believe they are. I need you to make a plan to improve." I was caught completely off-guard. I couldn't say it had been entirely smooth sailing, but I *was* starting to feel more confident and more at home in the role. If my performance was so bad, why hadn't my supervisor said anything yet? Why did I need a plan to do the work I was already doing? But I didn't want to risk the job I had worked so hard to get.

The following week, I walked into my boss's office and asked her if things were really going that poorly. She said (and I'll never forget this), "I'm *so* glad you finally said something." The look on her face was sheer relief. I, however, was stunned. Like you do in moments of panic, I played back scenes and conversations from my time in the role. No one had ever pointed out any deficiencies in my work. There was nothing in my personnel file. I had never been written up or put on performance plans, and at my check-ins there had never been any indication that I wasn't doing my job. Yet here she was, *so* relieved that I was finally coming to terms with a reality that no one had ever shared with me.

In that moment the reality of my role, my performance, and my environment all became much clearer to me: I believed I was doing well while all along the people who were supposed to be my support system were silently—willingly—watching me fail. Now that someone had said something, the problem became visible to me, and I knew I had to do something about it.

If you were failing and didn't realize it, wouldn't you want someone to tell you? If you came back from lunch with spinach in your teeth, would you want a colleague to pull you aside so you didn't embarrass yourself in front of an important client? This book is my telling you that you have spinach in your teeth. It's my telling you that you wore lipstick under your mask and now it's smeared all over your face. It's my telling you that in the face of heightened awareness, greater participation, and increased attention after George Floyd's murder, the racism and inequity that were present in 2020 are still present in 2023. Companies may talk about diversity more, and many individuals have participated in some form of DEIAA (Diversity, Equity, Inclusion, Accessibility, and Antiracism) training at work or hired people in DEIAA roles, but the needle isn't moving much. It's my telling you that a large percentage of organizations that made commitments immediately following George Floyd's murder have not actually followed through on those promises or are divesting from their DEIAA programs altogether. And people are already expressing fatigue from taking action for a few years and exhibiting less commitment as time goes on. It's my telling you, reader, that we have to behave differently and acknowledge the problems we have and that we know are wrong. Not enough work has been done and not enough conversations have been had for us to back away from our efforts; there is still a lot of progress to make. It's my telling you that in 2023, leaders can't move through the world while remaining as uninformed as they've been until now. Where we are today requires every person to accept personal responsibility if we are going to change our collective outcomes.

The reality is that we—all of us, but especially white folks themselves—have historically allowed white folks to fail on issues of racial inequity. They have been allowed to not show up, to opt in or out whenever they feel like it, or to just sit idly on the sidelines, not engaging when they see injustices happen. Now I've made you aware—and I know I'm not the first person to make you aware. Now that you know, you can do something about it. Maybe you're as shocked and stunned as I was when someone finally said to me, "You're not doing a good job." So, I'm that person who'll tell you, "You're not doing a good job. You can do better. Let's make a plan to improve." If I can transform from a broken person who lost a great deal of time and energy, even a good chunk of my hair, after that job experience because nobody would tell me the truth, you can transform into a person who's actively engaged around issues of race relations. And you can make a difference.

Now that you know, transformation is possible. You can move from ally to accomplice.

I believe that the work of becoming an accomplice and creating inclusive environments starts when individuals examine and improve their personal emotional intelligence and self-awareness. Individuals make up teams, and teams make up organizations. When I go into organizations and try to engage with the whole, someone in the space is inevitably thinking to themselves, *You know who should be here right now… Rachel. She definitely needs to hear this.* The reality is that no, YOU are Rachel and YOU need to be here.

This book is about the work you can do to lead in ways that create more inclusive outcomes and environments at work and beyond. It's a collection of information, prompts, and specific actions that you can bring into your life to grow into an accomplice and to develop antiracist practices. I will not convince you that racism exists. Instead, I will focus on the question "So what now?" *Racism exists and has for centuries, so what now? I know it's a problem, so what now?* This book is not a history lesson, though I share some history. I include details based on researchers' data, but I don't include every statistic. If you require or desire it, that data is out there for you to reference. But I'm not going to work that hard to convince you that those things are true. I'd rather spend my time and energy on moving to action. And last, this book is not a blueprint—we each have to participate, grow, and evolve in deeply personal ways.

Immediately after I quit the job I described above—which turned out to be slowly killing me—I told myself, "While this is where you are at this moment, you don't have to stay here." That is true for you as well. If you're sad, scared, distraught, or discouraged by the state of things, now is the time to opt in. Don't squander that energy on wallowing. These low times can also be the entry points to opportunity: an opportunity to do more and be more. I mean, if we're being honest with ourselves, we can only go up from here, right?!

This book isn't only for white people; it's for anyone who wants to be an accomplice and show up at work in ways that make the spaces around them more welcoming and engaging for all types of people. *From Ally to Accomplice* is for anyone who wants to use whatever power and privilege they have for the benefit of others.

If you're a white person, it will help you to:
- Identify how you are falling short on your journey and give you practices to overcome that.

- Understand how to engage in difficult conversations and circumstances and be less fearful about taking antiracist action.

- Lean into who you are and behaviors you're already doing to become a more equitable leader.

- Develop the confidence that you need to be an antiracist accomplice who can lead kick-ass companies and teams.

If you're BIPOC, it will help you to:

- Understand how you can show up as your authentic self and determine how you want to engage with your workplace's antiracism efforts.

- Grow the confidence to speak up and support other BIPOC colleagues.

- Give a framework and vocabulary to engage with folks who are trying to do antiracist work *and* to help folks who bring racist behaviors to work see the impact of their choices.

- Contend with the fact that racism and anti-Blackness are different, and anti-Blackness is sometimes stronger than racism, even for non-Black people of color .

- Inform your work culture in whatever way you choose.

Additional notes for BIPOC:

- Take from this book what you need and use it in whatever manner works best for you.

- Stay hydrated.

- Practice aggressive self-care.

Whoever you are, let me be clear: the book is not the work. For decades, many of us have observed people talking or reading about racism and race but not doing anything to change the realities of our circumstances. Reading this book won't change anything unless you then do something different. Having a book club conversation is not the work. If you think reading alone suddenly makes you an instant accomplice, put this book down right now. Yes. Right now. You are not considering how complex, personal, and ongoing this work will be.

Consistently moving to action with the information I share is the work. Nothing less.

ABOUT OUR JOURNEY

You want to increase your understanding and commitment to antiracism, so I will assume you are not new to this topic. I also assume that I don't need to convince you of a few things, like:

- Racism is real and harmful.

- Racism harms Black people disproportionately more than other historically underrepresented identities. Because of racism, anti-Blackness, and my own racial identity, I center the Black experience in this book.

- Dismantling the status quo requires everyone's participation—especially white people who hold systemic power in the United States.

- We must start creating more equitable places and spaces *now*.

If you take issue with these statements, you need a more basic book that will walk you through history, data, and lived experiences until you understand these truths.

Throughout this book I will share stories, histories, and facts that might be new to you or challenge what you have learned or experienced. I know we're strangers, but I am asking you to think about who you are and how you show up in the world. Wrestle with that a bit. Race and racial inequity can be uncomfortable topics, but if we don't talk about them, we will never reach a better understanding of who we are as members of society and how we each move through the world. No leader, manager, or colleague will be an accomplice and develop inclusive spaces unless they face the history and reality of BIPOC lived experiences.

On our journey, I will make very pointed connections about being an accomplice at work. But I weave together personal and professional stories and experiences to illustrate the necessity of the whole-person approach, and to encourage you to reframe your understanding of DEIAA work as more than a professional initiative. We each have so much unpacking to do and so much to rearrange and fix if we are going to live and lead in new ways. We have to ask, "What are the specific actions I can take in my life to create the world I want to live in?" And then we have to take those actions. We each have a sphere of influence in our personal and professional lives and in our communities, and we each have interests and talents we can put to good use. How can you lend your talents to a cause? How can you share your antiracist journey and reasons for starting it with people in your life? This is how we change our collective circumstances: all of us engaging in intentional actions to increase equity.

We don't have time to play games if we're serious about making a difference. I ask that you lean into any discomfort you might feel as you take in this book. I ask that you be curious and opt in. Those activities are the work as much as any activism or volunteerism is. If the book pisses you off or makes you mad, I'm okay with that. We don't need to be best friends. But take some time to really dig into your feelings. Sit with them. Hell, throw the book across the room if you need to, but examine that reaction and be truthful about it with yourself.

And here is where I say that it is okay: You can do this work. What's great about this process is that when you opt in, become antiracist, and commit to creating equitable and inclusive cultures, your outcomes and perspective change. You will be a better leader and citizen of the world when you become a better listener who more deeply interrogates policies, procedures, and ways of being you may have previously taken for granted. You will have a better understanding of how racism shapes the lives of everyone around you. You will possess a new lens and a new understanding of how race informs the world we live in and how racism stifles progress at every turn. You will also become more aware that injustice can be found in most places and then constantly seek it out and create more equitable circumstances. And, ultimately, you will have less discomfort and fear, and a greater ability to make change because you now know how to engage around the hardest topic to discuss: race.

Failure is hard to admit, especially when you feel like you don't own it all by yourself. With some space and time from my struggling job experience, I realized that I had never been given a plan for what success would look like in my role or the tools that would have helped me succeed. Poor communication and unclear expectations plagued my tenure. My supervisor obviously didn't help direct my efforts to align with the unspoken expectations. In fact, as I floundered for months, the distance between the team and me seemed to expand; the only element that grew was distrust. What's funny is that I was spending so much time spinning in the work that I didn't know I was floundering. In hindsight, many factors contributed to my failure, including a leader who wasn't able to guide and support a Black woman in her role.

That place was the last straw after a series of job experiences filled with microaggressions and racism. I once had a colleague tell me, "You've gotta stop talking about racism and being Black." He was essentially telling me that I should leave an integral part of my identity at the door even though I was the only person of color on staff in a leadership role and the organization claimed to be working to be more inclusive. I had a colleague frequently try to empathize with me by saying that he understood what I went through as a Black woman because his husband was Mexican. This ignores the difference between people who choose to immigrate to a place and those brought to a place without consent. I also had coworkers come into my office and write on my whiteboard alternate phrases for me to use because they believed "There's a nicer way to say that." Read that again: They entered my office and suggested different ways to speak to them and others in our workplace! As the only person of color in the department and one of four in a staff of more than 150 people, I believe they thought they were helping me acculturate into their workplace, but what I really needed was them to allow me to speak and behave as I was. All to say, I have been surrounded by people failing to even try to understand how to support or respectfully interact with Black people in the workplace.

Finally leaving that job, and the corporate workforce altogether, saved my life. I was tired of working in spaces where I felt so crappy, unsupported, and unchampioned. I knew that I wanted—and needed—to create something better for myself and hopefully others. It was then, at one of my lowest moments, when I doubted my skills and my purpose, that I finally opted in to antiracist work with everything I had. I knew I couldn't go back into *any* workplace in which I had to hide, protect, or compromise any part of me. So, I started my own company and built a brand and business from scratch. It wasn't easy, but as I did it, I remembered how smart and capable I was. And as I regained energy, confidence, and focus within my own workspace, I realized just how toxic those previous work environments had been for me. I experienced work trauma. Everyone around me watching me struggling, and no one throwing me a lifejacket, was the last straw. Sure, I wasn't struggling in a dramatic way, but not all struggles are loud and raucous and not all trauma is caused by a specific flash of violence with blood everywhere. Sometimes trauma grows out of smaller, quieter moments of being treated as if no one cares if you sink or swim. Trauma can fester when you're not treated as a peer, when people know and recognize that and still do nothing. I was showing up every day with passion, talent, intelligence, a smile, a bubbly personality, and effort, and that energy was stomped out of me before the end of every workday. Now, when I go into companies and meet with teams, I am very aware that toxicity and trauma can be present even when everyone is smiling. I know because I lived it.

I engage in the work of creating equitable and inclusive environments and circumstances to ensure that other BIPOC don't have to endure what I endured at so many jobs. I can't say that how I was treated throughout my career was definitely racist; I can't say that it wasn't. What I do know is that job conditions were not set up for me to succeed, and people did not know how to interact with some very basic and important aspects of me and my identity. Perhaps my former colleagues didn't know what I needed or how to help me. Maybe my supervisors didn't have a full picture of what success (for both of us) would look like. Yet optimal conditions are what every leader and workplace should be diligently working to create. In fact, that should be one of the highest priorities. Organizations can do this by approaching conditions with a racial equity lens because who needs what and how much will depend on the person, their background, and their lived experience. Truly, a leader can only be effective, and should only feel successful, if they are willing to create optimal conditions for *every* employee.

A Black woman colleague who was at the same level as me at that company has now ascended to high heights there. I have no doubt that she will one day run the organization if she so desires. The only difference between her experience and mine was that her boss supported her. My colleague was given a clear path and opportunities to lead and lean into her strengths. She experienced a level of transparency and support that was never made available to me. Now let's be clear: I am not bitter. Without that experience, I would not be where I am today. We are both very smart, competent, badass humans, but having a leader who championed her helped ensure an entirely different outcome. As you engage with this book, my question for you is: Which leader do you want to be?

ON EXPERIENCE AND LANGUAGE

This book is a reflection of my personal lived experiences. In writing this book, I strive to honor the experiences and stories shared with me by real people who have faced the issues I raise. There are many, though all names have been changed to protect the innocent and the guilty. I have been doing this work for a long time, and the situations and conversations discussed here repeat themselves. Take the stories for what they are: my attempt to shed light on the truths of our circumstances.

Throughout the book, I have done my best to avoid ableist or problematic language, and yet I'm sure someone will find instances in these pages. Language evolves and is imperfect at best. The terms we use to label or identify people, practices, concepts, ideas, and behaviors change constantly.

I am not a fan of acronyms in general. However, in this book I use the term *BIPOC* as an acronym for those who identify as and/or are racialized as Black, Indigenous, and people of color. It typically refers to all people who are not white. While it's a recognizable shorthand, it also presents a challenge that I want to call out. First, there is great nuance in each of these communities. People who fall under this umbrella term face very different challenges, and I've worked to provide context when and where I can. Second, a lot of BIPOC want to learn, and need to learn, to be accomplices. Not all BIPOC are living an accomplice lifestyle. I see BIPOC uphold white supremacy as offensively as white people through their actions. I also know that some white folks live as full-fledged accomplices. We are all at different points on our journey.

Throughout the book, I will also use specific terms such as *Black*, *Indigenous*, or *Asian*. While these are general categories, they break down BIPOC into groups with more similar (though not monolithic) racialized experiences. My assumption is that Black people have a pretty good handle on racism and antiracism; other BIPOC may have less of a handle on it if their experiences aren't compounded by anti-Blackness; or—because of their lived experiences—white people generally don't have a true handle on race (even if you are married to Black person or have adopted an Asian child). These general groups are the audiences for this book, and I will speak to each with those assumptions built in. These assumptions are based on my own lived experience, and yet, I know they are assumptions. When I use this specific language, remember all the small but meaningful differences that still exist among people, even if I'm not mentioning them all every time.

The same slipperiness is true of DEIAA (diversity, equity, inclusion, accessibility, and antiracism) work, which is also sometimes called DEI, DE&I, D&I, IDEA, DEIA, DEIJ, DEIJA, DEIB, or EDI work. When I use *DEIAA* I'm talking about all of the above: efforts that include diversity, inclusion, equity, justice, belonging, accessibility, and antiracism for all people in all spaces. In a year all of these terms might be outdated and replaced by something else. About ten years ago we lived in a world where, when it came to gender, pronouns were often assumed, with only the binary *she* and *he* applied to everyone. Now, the list of pronouns—and all of the words by which we identify ourselves—has expanded tremendously, and we commonly identify our pronouns on LinkedIn, at conferences, and in email signatures. Our language and the practices around it have evolved. The same will be true for terminology about race and racial identity.

I share this for two reasons: First, to acknowledge that any terms I use here when referring to the race and skin experience of people in this country are limiting and may have an expiration date. Second, because whatever language you use or get comfortable with will require you to adapt at some point. Don't get attached to the specific words used to make sense of the ideas in this book or of race more generally. Use the words to understand the concepts and the ideas, and then know that it will all evolve. We're humans: it's what we do as we learn about ourselves and the world. It's been happening for centuries, and it will continue. This is a lifelong journey, and language is a piece of that work.

Finally, at times you might disagree with me. Know that I stand by what is written here. In other words, "I said what I said."

With Joy,
Seena

CHAPTER 1: WE NEED ACCOMPLICES

Get Woke, Stay Woke

"What would an accomplice do?" I hope you consistently ask yourself that question at every turn after you read this book. So, what better way to start our journey together than looking at one example of what an accomplice does?

A few months ago, I was sitting in a group leadership session with one of my clients, James, a white vice president of fulfillment for a large multinational corporation, as he faced a situation that challenged how he understood his role in making change. A day prior to our meeting, Thomas, a Black warehouse employee, had gone to a nearby café to grab lunch during the workday. The café was a common destination for many of the warehouse employees, and the people working there knew Thomas by name. On this particular day, as Thomas was choosing what to order, a white man walked into the store and asked who was parked in the handicapped parking space out front. Thomas had parked with all the proof that he was allowed to use the space (his permit was visibly displayed), and he told the other customer so. Somehow that wasn't enough. The gentleman challenged and questioned Thomas again and would not stop. During the extensive back and forth, Thomas had to continually defend his right to be in the parking spot while the other man continually chastised him, and no one in the store did anything to shut down the absurd line of questioning. Thomas sped up his ordering, paid, and exited the store. But it didn't end there. The accoster followed him out to his car, harassing Thomas and making monkey gestures.[1]

When Thomas got back to his shift, he told his supervisor that he wasn't in the right frame of mind to keep working and asked for the rest of the day off. When the supervisor asked if he was okay, Thomas—who was visibly upset—explained what had happened over lunch. Understandably, the supervisor agreed that Thomas should take space and go home. The supervisor immediately went to his boss, my client James, and relayed what happened.

So here we were in our leadership coaching session, with James sitting at a conference table and telling all the other executives Thomas's story. As he finished sharing, everyone around the table expressed sympathy with Thomas. They nodded and acknowledged the difficulty of just letting go and getting back to a to-do list after such a jarring incident. After I listened to their conversation, I reminded them of why they hired me and that engaging as an accomplice means doing the work of changing situations and circumstances, not just talking about situations and circumstances. Heads nodded.

Then I asked, "What are you going to do, now that you know Thomas went through that at a business that many of your employees patronize?"

The executives looked at each other, and one said, "Can we do anything?" They started listing excuses that many leaders use to avoid taking action, like "Well, it didn't happen at our place of business" and "We don't know anyone at the café!" I followed with, "Here is what you can do. You can call the café, tell them what happened to Thomas, and explain that you will discourage your employees from going there if the café's management doesn't do something about this."

Now, I realize this was a terrifying proposition for a handful

---

[1] There is a long history of scientific racism, which includes likening Black people to monkeys and apes. The exact origin of that association is difficult to determine, but the trope is used negatively and in obviously insulting ways. The notion has its roots in the work of such people as Johann Blumenbach, Charles Darwin, and George Robins Gliddon and Josiah Clark Nott, authors of *Types of Mankind*.

of white leaders. They weren't accustomed to addressing a racist experience on someone else's behalf; in fact, they likely had never had to discuss race or a racial assault directly. As fledgling accomplices, they were just learning how to take intentional and purposeful action as it related to race. They were scared. They didn't want to mess up. But I knew that, as leaders of a global company, they had gone through difficult times before. They built a multi million-dollar business from scratch. They scaled and pivoted several times to carve out a place in their market, and they did all this in just twenty years. None of that was easy; it required learning and action along the way. Twenty years in, all of them were still highly competent individuals who could learn new skills and talents as needed. But this kind of tough conversation was unique and risky to them. I empathize with that, but I was also clear about what needed to happen.

This was a defining moment for James and the entire team. Out loud, they asked themselves, "Can we go as far as Seena is suggesting?" But the quieter question they asked themselves, and that raised a little bit of fear in each of them, was, "Am I an ally or am I an accomplice?"

In our next session, I followed up with the team. James had talked to Thomas about what happened and made it clear to him that the company was going to have his back. James then picked up the phone and called the café. James said to the manager, "We feel very serious about antiracism as a company, and recently one of our employees was accosted by another customer at your place of business. While it happened, no one said anything or supported our employee, so now we have an obligation to get involved. My expectation is that you do more when things like this happen on your premises." The manager apologized and even acknowledged that he himself was there when this all went down. James said, "I am going to bring Thomas over, and I want you to apologize to him."

When Thomas and James arrived, the manager said, "The business should have done more and been more proactive. And as an individual, I should have done better." Thomas and James then grabbed lunch (on the house) and headed back to the company. They ended up having a two-hour conversation in which they shared their personal life stories and also discussed other incidents like this. Thomas explained, "This may seem extraordinary to you, but things like this happen to me all the time."

My guess is that placing that first call to the café was hard for James: not knowing exactly what to say, how it was going to all turn out, or even if he was going to do any actual good. But that call didn't nearly equate to how hard it was for Thomas to be racialized and confronted while simply trying to buy a soft drink.

In the end, the rewards for engaging as accomplices, for speaking up and taking action, far outweighed the initial fear and risk. When I reflect on some of the outcomes, these come to mind:

- The leadership team used their power and privilege on behalf of someone with less power and showed Thomas (and other employees) that they actually had his back.

- They risked their comfort and business relationships to make their work environment more equitable for Thomas and the rest of the staff.

- They modeled empathetic, antiracist behavior within their team and for another business in their community.

- The episode spurred more and deeper team conversations among James, Thomas, and their colleagues about lived experiences and how to support each other at work and beyond.

- It catalyzed discussion between leadership and staff about the ways individuals can shape the culture of the organization.

- James moved beyond the fear he experienced when faced with the prospect of moving to action around the circumstance.

- James expanded his capabilities around unfamiliar and difficult conversations. In fact, he reported feeling more willing and able to have career-risking conversations if that's what it took to support others around him.

These actions toward equity grew connection, loyalty, and personal skills. But more than that, they created a better environment for Thomas and other BIPOC employees at his workplace. Thomas can now bring more of himself and his personal experience to work because he has witnessed that it's acceptable to share his racialized experiences with his colleagues and, importantly, his boss. No one doubted him or asked him to prove his story. His manager listened to him and took action based on what he heard. This incident and how Thomas handled it made it possible for his BIPOC colleagues to have deeper conversations about their personal experiences at work, too. And James made himself accountable to correct a wrong that he didn't commit because it was the right thing to do. This is what leading as a fierce accomplice can look and feel like for a leader, a team, and an organization.

This story illustrates what we are working toward together in this book: **Inclusive environments in which BIPOC can be their whole selves at work and white colleagues are not afraid to act when it comes to inequities and know how to be effective accomplices at work.** James and Thomas didn't dismantle everything that's wrong in our world in one fell swoop, but their situation did demonstrate an honest, challenging, and hopeful look at what being an accomplice requires and its impact on real-world circumstances across an organization. I hope the example assuages the fear that you may have about not knowing what equity and inclusion look like in action.

You don't have to do entirely new or different things to achieve equitable and inclusive spaces, but you *do* have to approach the world and your work with a different set of practices. In this chapter, I'll share what accomplices are, how they behave, and why they are crucial for changing our circumstances. Spending time on these definitions, explanations, and reflections is, as you will see, all part of the work of being an accomplice: someone who takes time to understand the process and develop a practice, instead of jumping straight to "Okay, but what do I *do*?!"

> To get us started, let's look at a definition of allyship:
>
> Allyship is well-intentioned behavior in support of members of historically excluded groups. It is not an identity one can claim. The distinction of allyship can only be bestowed by those we seek to support. Allies take direction from members of underrepresented groups. Allies' engagement is often rooted in listening and learning, but they can find it hard to move to action. While allies act from a place of wanting to help others and be "good people," they do not feel a personal responsibility to change others' circumstances.

Let's explore what these phrases and sentences mean.

Allyship is not an identity one can claim.
You don't get to call yourself an ally; only others can say you are one. If asked, do you think individuals from historically underrepresented groups would call you an ally? If you take honest stock of what you're doing to support others, do you feel like you're doing what others want and need you to do? I'm asking you these questions not to make you feel bad, but simply to encourage self-awareness of what you are and are not doing. After working with thousands of people, I can say that almost no one is doing enough for folks from historically underrepresented groups.

Allies' engagement is often rooted in listening and learning, but they can find it hard to move to action.
In the wake of the racial uprisings of 2020, I often witnessed white people using the refrain "I'm listening" when engaging with content or experiences shared by people of color. The thing is, listening is not enough, and it's often used as an excuse *not* to move to action. Listening will change nothing about our moment. Listening and learning are significant steps and critical to engaging responsibly, but moving to action based on what you hear and learn is what will lead us to different outcomes. Staying in the learning zone usually makes an ally feel comfortable and knowledgeable without the discomfort of doing something with what they know or putting themselves in new situations.

Allies act from a place of wanting to help others and be "good people."
Allies often act from a place of wanting to help but not seeing themselves as change agents or as truly responsible for making changes toward a more equitable society. It's not bad to want to help others, but the goal isn't to help them; the goal is to change the circumstances and situations that create and perpetuate inequity. Help implies power—me helping you—and "helping" often sticks to the symptoms of deeper, lingering problems instead of addressing their roots: serving hot meals instead of challenging housing inequity, donating money to nonprofits instead of mutual-aid funds. Such well-intentioned behaviors can verge on white saviorism. *White saviors* are "those who work from the assumption that they know best what BIPOC folks need. They believe it's their responsibility to support and uplift communities of color—in their own country or somewhere else—because people of color lack the resources, willpower, and intelligence to do it themselves."[2] While we aren't

---

[2] "A Savior No One Needs: Unpacking and Overcoming the White Savior Complex," *Healthline*, accessed July 29th, 2022, https://www.healthline.com/health/white-saviorism#examples.

necessarily talking about Western versus non-Western nations in this book, the concept remains relevant. If we lead with helping, we assume that we are in a dominant or more knowledgeable role and stop short of real change. The white savior believes that people want the same thing that they would want or need in any given situation. Oftentimes, that is not the case.

DEIAA WORK IS NOT ABOUT SAVING PEOPLE; IT'S ABOUT DISMANTLING SYSTEMS.

BIPOC don't personally need your help; we simply want to operate on a level playing field. I assure you that we will do just fine once that happens. Some of us are already thriving in spite of the current racist climate.

Allies are "good people" who sometimes help others but do not consistently disrupt the status quo. They may be aware of how pervasive racism is but be overwhelmed into inaction because that reality is so much to take in.

I ALWAYS SAY, "ONCE YOU SEE INJUSTICE, YOU CANNOT UNSEE IT."

The amount of injustice in the world can overwhelm people. It is a lot. In fact, BIPOC have been saying that for decades.

Most people are allies in my definition of the word. People will throw on a T-shirt with the words *I'm an Ally*, and that's the extent of their allyship. Do you remember in 2016 when there was a brief "movement" of people wearing safety pins on their jackets as a representation of their allyship to, well, basically all people who have historically been pushed to the margins? Many people, often white people, donned these pins to signal that they were a "safe" space for the people who were being targeted by violence after Donald Trump won the presidential election. Shortly after the pin movement gained momentum, people from those underrepresented communities rightly designated it as "slacktivism."[3] Why? Come on! I think we all know why: The people who put on the pins often did nothing else to ensure others' safety. This kind of performative and optical allyship is rampant. From the black squares people shared on Instagram on June 2, 2020, in solidarity with #blackouttuesday to the Black Lives Matter statements companies post after a Black person is murdered by law enforcement. That performativity doesn't feel safe for us because it prevents us from knowing who we can trust.

To play and win the game, you have to know who is actually on your team, the roles you each perform, and that you can count on everyone showing up on the field. If an entire team wants to wear the jersey just because they're fashionable or in their favorite color, you won't make the championship. When you don't know who is on your team, it's possible that no one will show up to play. Or, worse, they show up and then let the other team win because they're not really invested. This unpredictable game plays out daily when people say they support BIPOC but then don't show up for us.

The upside is that allies do see what is going on in our world. They are not ignorant of what's happening; they have just not found a sustainable way to contribute to changing it—to suit up and play the game.

So, what is an accomplice and what makes them different from allies?

> Accompliceship is a proactive practice of ongoing learning and continuous action in relation to what one learns. It is not an identity; it's intentional, antiracist behavior derived from awareness and

---

[3] Alex Abad-Santos, "The Backlash over Safety Pins and Allies, Explained," November 17, 2016, https://www.vox.com/culture/2016/11/17/13636156/safety-pins-backlash-trump-brexit.

understanding and informed by those you seek to serve. Accomplices feel a personal responsibility to rectify the historical effects and current realities of historically underrepresented people's oppression. They take action, educate themselves, and risk their power and privilege for the benefit of others to create a more equitable and just society.

That sounds fierce, right? I know!

Accompliceship is a proactive practice of ongoing learning and continuous action.
Being an accomplice is a practice, which, like anything you are striving to develop, requires a great deal of repetition and consistency. This means that one day you might behave in a way that fully supports a person from a historically excluded group and the next day you might mess up. That fact makes this terrifying for some people, especially perfectionists and those who aren't used to making mistakes. But it's part of this journey. An empowering and forgiving mental reframing when you mess up is to say to yourself: "I get to keep trying." Every time you are called in for an error, perceive that as a favor someone is doing by helping you be a more informed and more empathetic person.

It is not an identity; it's intentional, antiracist behavior derived from awareness and understanding . . .
I use "intentional behavior" in direct contrast to "well-intentioned" allyship. Well-intentioned behavior credits good intentions despite the outcomes. Allies' behavior is often off the mark because it derives from the subject's perspective, not the object's or the receiving party's perspective. For example, the colleagues who invaded my office to tell me "better" ways of speaking or the colleague who told me that he understood my lived experience because his husband was Mexican

had good intentions—do you think they stopped to think about the outcome of their actions from my perspective?

For an accomplice, antiracist behavior is intentional: deliberate and purposeful. Antiracist behavior is acting in accordance with the belief that the concept of race impacts our lived experiences and is the issue that most prevents progress. If you're not actively working against racism, you're implicitly supporting it. When your behavior is both intentional and antiracist, your actions are deliberately rooted in an awareness and understanding of race and racism.

. . . and informed by those you seek to serve.

When you're acting as an accomplice, your awareness and decisions are not all about you, instead they are driven by the needs and voices of those you are serving. If you're not actively seeking out the perspectives and opinions of the people you want to serve, there is zero chance that you will be effective.

Accomplices feel a personal responsibility to rectify the historical effects and current realities of the oppression of historically underrepresented people.

Every person, regardless of racial identity, can be an accomplice. Accomplices know the history and are not discouraged or overwhelmed by it. They take responsibility. The fact that we are in this situation, that the data in every industry and every sector shows that there is no level playing field for BIPOC, is all accomplices need to know to take responsibility for doing the work to make much needed progress.

They take action, educate themselves, and risk their power and privilege for the benefit of others to create a more equitable and just society.

You must be active to engage as an accomplice; you can't be passive. You are either disrupting the status quo or actively planning how to disrupt it. You challenge the systems, structures, and circumstances that don't serve folks who are historically underrepresented. In other words, you actively seek to change aspects of the dominant culture. Taking action is what distinguishes practitioners from performers.

Accomplices hold it down. Period. They don't care if anyone labels them an "ally" or an "accomplice." They care about the work and about improving the state of things. Imagine running a marathon. An ally would be on the sidelines, handing you water at a few hydration stations along the way. An accomplice would be running the race alongside you, pouring water into your mouth and encouraging you the whole distance, watching for potholes, even moving things out of your way! They would make sure you finish the doggone race because they know how much you trained for that moment and how much it means to you.

Accomplices are self-aware. They know they don't know everything and have a lot to learn from the people they seek to serve. They're okay with this and take their cues from those very people—they let others lead. They acknowledge that others have a valid and different understanding of the world and know their place. This self-awareness comes from education: They've taught themselves to engage in and be familiar with the key issues and how we got here.

THE MORE YOU KNOW, THE BETTER EQUIPPED YOU ARE TO ENGAGE IN AN UNCOMFORTABLE SITUATION.

Think about buying a new vacuum or coffee maker. After a certain age, many people refuse to look at the manual for a bright, shiny new appliance. They think, "How hard can using a vacuum be?" An accomplice reads the manual. They aren't just winging it. The same is true in how they show up for others: They read up on the topics, get familiar with the terminology, and learn what actions to take.

This table compares the ways allies and accomplices think and act. As you read it, compare these actions to how you might be thinking and acting and how you might move toward accompliceship.

Allyship is a set of practices that support historically underrepresented groups. Allies:	Accompliceship is an antiracist way of being that serves historically underrepresented groups. Accomplices:
Work on issues, but not with an antiracist lens	Center race when engaging with issues
Are willing to change things	Know they are responsible for changing things
Acknowledge their power and privilege	Use their power and privilege for the benefit of others
Show up on their own terms (when it's convenient, easy, or helpful to them)	Opt in every day regardless of their own personal circumstances
Think of antiracism as something they do when it suits a particular circumstance	Integrate antiracism into who they are
Believe in antiracist ideas	Exhibit antiracist behaviors
Are collaborators	Are partners
Believe inequity exists	Seek to make situations equitable
Expect to learn from BIPOC	Follow the lead of BIPOC and create communities/cultures of learning with other white folks

Talk about the issues	Take action on the issues
Are willing to be uncomfortable	Disavow the desire or right to be comfortable all the time
Take orders	Know where they fit in, when to act, and when to listen
Recognize and acknowledge damaging situations	Take risks to address damaging situations
Labor for recognition or praise	Labor on behalf of others
Know where we're at as it relates to racial equity	Know *how we got* to the place we're at with racial inequity
Empathize with where we're at with racial inequity	Empathize with the people who are affected by racial inequity
Need direction in antiracist behaviors, actions, and learning (reactive)	Are self-sufficient in antiracist behaviors, actions, and learning (proactive)
Believe in "doing the right thing"	Believe we have a moral imperative to take action when circumstances are not equitable
Can let guilt or overwhelm stop them from taking action	Know to pause, consider, and then react
React from a place of defensiveness	Can identify and move past their defensiveness or overwhelm to take action

When people honestly contemplate the differences between these behaviors, I observe that they often feel guilt, fear, sadness, and disappointment with themselves. It can be an "oh crap" moment because, when pressed, they understand that thinking is not the same as doing—that wanting equity is not the same as working to make things equitable. Perhaps you're feeling some of this too. I want to pause to make space for these feelings because that's real, and yet that pause can't last. I want you to reframe any negative emotions or discomfort into a more substantial commitment to the work.

ACCOMPLICESHIP IS NECESSARY FOR LEADING IN THE TWENTY-FIRST CENTURY AND BEYOND

In school or at work, people learn all kinds of lessons, strategies, and skills to "be strong leaders" and climb those corporate ladders—commanding presence, making quick decisions, negotiating between parties. But they're never taught how to be effective accomplices. No one has been expected to support people from historically underrepresented groups on their own terms. Until now. The ability to bring race-based empathy and knowledge of historical and current events related to race is necessary for every leader from now forward. The world is changing, and business—and the people working in businesses—will change right alongside it. Let's take a look at some demographic realities and predictions.

According to the 2020 US Census, BIPOC currently constitute the majority of the population in California, Texas, Hawaii, Nevada, Maryland, and New Mexico. BIPOC in Arizona, Florida, Georgia, Louisiana, Mississippi, New Jersey, and New York make up more than 40 percent of the population. Using the 2020 data, the US Census Bureau predicts that by the year 2044, the United States will have no clear racial or ethnic majority. According to the new population projections:

- Whites will make up 49.7 percent of the population, followed by Latinos at 25 percent, African Americans at 12.7 percent, and Asians at 7.9 percent. Approximately 4 percent of the population will be multiracial.

- The multiracial population was measured at 9 million people in 2010 and at 33.8 million people in 2020, a 276 percent increase.

- The white adult population (age 18 and over) went from 74.7 percent in 2010 to 64.1 percent in 2020. In contrast, the multiracial adult population increased from 2.1 percent in 2010 to 8.8 percent in 2020.

The nation's workforce is becoming increasingly diverse. In the forty years between 1980 and 2020, the white working-age population declined from 83 percent of the nation's total to 63 percent, while the number of historically underrepresented workers doubled. Extrapolating from 2010 to 2030, BIPOC will represent the largest share of workforce growth and will account for 120 percent of total net workforce growth. The share of total net growth in the Hispanic/Latino workforce is expected to be the highest of all racial and ethnic groups, reaching close to 78 percent. The people who will be working for you, including your leadership team, will be predominantly nonwhite—if your workforce reflects the actual US population. And, in advance of the 2020 census results, the US Census Bureau released race-ethnic population estimates showing that, in 2019, "for the first time, more than half of the nation's population under age 16 identified as a racial or ethnic minority. Among this group, Latino or Hispanic and Black residents together comprise nearly 40 percent of the population."[4]

As the demographics change, attitudes and perspectives about what people need and want to thrive at work are changing too. Millennials believe companies should be actively involved in social issues, and two-thirds visit corporate websites at least somewhat

---

[4] William H. Frey "The Nation Is Diversifying Even Faster Than Predicted, According to New Census Data," July 1, 2020, https://www.brookings.edu/research/new-census-data-shows-the-nation-is-diversifying-even-faster-than-predicted/.

often to learn about their efforts.[5] And 90 percent of Gen Z believes companies must act to help social and environmental issues; 75 percent will do research to see if a company is being honest when it takes a stand on issues.[6] The Gen Z generation expects companies and leaders to have a consistent stance on issues that affect them and their world.

People care about the culture at their workplaces. A 2021 study found that 60 percent of the surveyed Americans would take a job they love with half their current income over a job they hated that doubled their current income.[7] The 2017 *What People Want Report* by Hays US, a recruitment agency, found that culture is the main reason people would consider leaving their current role, with 34 percent overall listing it as the main motivator and 47 percent of active job seekers saying it is the reason they are leaving their current role.[8]

Of course people care about culture, but maybe you're wondering whether *inclusive* culture actually influences the decision to leave a company. Yes. A McKinsey study from 2021 found that the top three factors employees cited as reasons for quitting were: didn't feel valued by their organizations (54 percent); didn't feel valued by their managers (52 percent); didn't feel a sense of belonging at work (51 percent).[9] And a Columbia University study by Michael Slepian and Drew Jacoby-Senghor found, "When employees felt like they didn't belong in the workplace, they felt like they couldn't be themselves at work. When employees feel they can't be their authentic self at work, they have lower workplace satisfaction, find less meaning in their work, and have one foot out the door."[10] A 2022 study published in

---

[5] https://pointsoflight.org/civic-engagement-research/

[6] https://www.conecomm.com/research-blog/cone-gen-z-purpose-study

[7] "Study: Americans would take a 50% pay cut for a job they really love," March 19, 2021, https://www.lexingtonlaw.com/blog/news/employee-happiness.html.

[8] *What People Want* report, Hays, accessed June 6th, 2022, https://www.hays.com/resources/what-people-want-2017.

[9] Aaron De Smet, Bonnie Dowling, Marino Mugayar-Baldocchi, and Bill Schaninger, "'Great Attrition' or 'Great Attraction'? The choice is yours," McKinsey, September 8, 2021, https://www.mckinsey.com/business-functions/people-and-organizational-performance/our-insights/great-attrition-or-great-attraction-the-choice-is-yours.

[10] Michael Slepian, "Are Your D&I Efforts Helping Employees Feel Like They Belong?" *Harvard Business Review*, August, 19, 2020, https://hbr.org/2020/08/are-your-di-efforts-helping-employees-feel-like-they-belong.

the *MIT Sloan Management Review* exploring the Great Resignation found, "A toxic corporate culture is by far the strongest predictor of industry-adjusted attrition and is ten times more important than compensation in predicting turnover. Our analysis found that the leading elements contributing to toxic cultures include failure to promote diversity, equity, and inclusion; workers feeling disrespected; and unethical behavior."[11]

And what do you get when you create a culture where people feel like they can be themselves? In a recent BetterUp study, the authors found that "high belonging was linked to a whopping 56 percent increase in job performance, a 50 percent drop in turnover risk, and a 75 percent reduction in sick days. For a 10,000-person company, this would result in annual savings of more than $52M."[12]

So here is what you now know: The workforce will be increasingly diverse moving forward; ensuring that all people feel like they belong in the workplace and work culture you create is key to retention and productivity; and people *will* stick around and do great work if they get what they need from their leaders, managers, and workspaces. Yet today I hear nearly the same comments repeatedly from BIPOC and white people about race and about work in particular that show me we are not prepared for what the next five to twenty years will necessitate.

BIPOC tell me:

- My colleagues want me to turn on my video camera in meetings the day after another Black person was murdered and highly publicized across the media.

- I can't tell my coworkers about the racism I experience at work without someone being offended.

---

[11] Donald Sull, Charles Sull, and Ben Zweig, "Toxic Culture Is Driving the Great Resignation," *MIT Sloan Management Review*, January 11, 2022, https://sloanreview.mit.edu/article/toxic-culture-is-driving-the-great-resignation/.

[12] Evan W. Carr, Andrew Reece, Gabriella Rosen Kellerman, and Alexi Robichaux, "The Value of Belonging at Work," *Harvard Business Review*, December 16, 2019, https://hbr.org/2019/12/the-value-of-belonging-at-work.

- I don't want to go back to the office full-time now that I've been working remotely; it's so much more comfortable to be at home and away from the typical casual racism at the office.
- I can't report microaggressions because I have no support or person to talk to about them.
- The DEIAA work that we are engaged in is performative at best. Nothing has changed.
- There are *still* no BIPOC senior leaders at our company.
- When I go to staff meetings and horrible situations have happened recently in the world, no one brings it up, so I feel like I can't bring it up even though I'm affected.

White people tell me:
- I wish someone would tell me what to do, and then I could just do it.
- I'm afraid I'm going to do or say the wrong thing.
- I'm afraid someone will get mad at me if I try to be antiracist or talk about the topic at work.
- I'm afraid if I bring up race or racism at work, I won't have the support of my leadership.
- I'm afraid my team won't want to do DEIAA work because they've never had to.
- I'm not sure how to plug DEIAA work into the broader organization.
- I know I want to do the right thing, but I'm not sure about X, Y, or Z.

These comments point very directly at two truths I've discovered after working with hundreds of folks: BIPOC can't bring their whole selves to work, and white people are afraid of messing up or have no idea how to be antiracist (which manifests as fear). At some point we have to meet in the middle. BIPOC have to advocate for what they need to show up as themselves, and white people need to move through their fear and prepare to take continuous equitable action. We need leaders who are courageous enough to create inclusive spaces and ensure BIPOC success in those spaces, which is what I didn't have in many of my previous organizations. I don't want BIPOC to face the situations I did, where no one spoke directly to me about our circumstance or people silenced a crucial part of my identity (my racial experience). Sometimes systemic racism allows these things to happen. We need leaders who will work their asses off to hire, promote, and retain BIPOC; sponsor them on their terms; partner and support them in all the ways they ask; believe them; positively mention their names in rooms they're not in; and ultimately see their full humanity.

Two key attributes of being an accomplice will chip away at the distance between the truths above: a fierce commitment to antiracism and risky behavior. Accomplices must address race, which is the hardest, longest-lasting problem in the United States. Race continues to erode our society, our relationships, and our workplaces because we don't center it in our problem solving, yet there is a direct throughline from our country's earliest racist founding and growth to nearly every problem we have today. Our racist past is a deep and complex reality that we as a collective refuse to address. We talk around it because it's too controversial to speak to it. And the fact is, until we speak directly to it, we'll never stop dealing indirectly about it.

Solving for race requires you view whatever business, social, or cultural problem you're tackling at work and in life through an antiracist lens—and there is *always* a racial component, inequity, or history to every issue. As an accomplice, when you do this you begin to disassemble the structures built to maintain the original hierarchy of power. If we are committed to being better people—if we are committed to building places and spaces with more equitable and inclusive policies and circumstances—we have to solve race first, and only then will we be able to solve other issues such as pay equity, reproductive rights, violence prevention, and access to healthcare, education, and housing.

And then risk. What is risk, really? Taking a risk, for our purposes, means that you're willing to leverage both your power and your privilege for the benefit of others. *Leverage* is an important word here. Leveraging is strategic; leveraging is using something to maximum advantage. How and where you leverage your power and privilege is something you must assess moment by moment. What you're often leveraging your existing comfort and familiarity in exchange for disrupting the status quo. You're risking what was for what can be, should be, or is possible.

As we think about leading and creating more inclusive environments, we realize that there is a lot of risk in changing the dominant culture; it can really rock the boat. There may be traditions, processes, or commonly used language that feel like second nature but are in fact exclusionary. Taking risks to address seemingly small but actually impactful ways of operating could look like:

- Sacrificing contracts with clients or vendors that are not in alignment with antiracist values.

- Adding more steps and processes to identify candidates and ensure inclusive hiring.

- Holding individuals accountable to antiracist and inclusive practices in annual reviews.

- Eliminate time-honored traditions and rituals that are non-inclusive or potentially offensive.

- Challenging your ego as a leader by engaging and listening to honest feedback from employees about the organizational work culture and making changes based on what you learn from them.

- Publishing language on the company or internal communication channels and in public-facing materials, like the website, that include antiracist values—and then living by them.

There are benefits to taking risks both professionally and personally. In business, risk correlates with innovation and greater creativity. When you start doing things differently, you discover more and more things that could be done differently. You approach obstacles with more energy because you have new skills around calculating risks, trying new things, and assessing outcomes. If you continue with "business as usual" you don't gain any of those benefits. On the personal front, when you take risks you gain confidence, learn new skills and information, increase opportunities to engage with the world around you, and develop emotional resilience. I know this may sound like armchair psychology, but I list these benefits because I've seen them in action for others and myself. I've learned to take more risks rooted in accompliceship as my business grows. I've navigated the "Is this going too far?" waters and reached the other side with more experience, more skill, and greater security in how I do this work. There's that old adage "you get out of it what you put into it." Bigger risk, bigger reward.

As I was writing this book, I was hired to present an hour-and-a-half-long virtual, interactive version of "From Ally to Accomplice" for attendees who opted into the breakout session at a conference. I prepared as I usually do, signed on, introduced myself, and started talking. I love talking about this work, I truly do. I love learning from others, sharing new information with people and hopefully broadening perspectives as I go. The talk went splendidly, with a lot of active participation, which I always perceive as a great success. After the attendees signed off, one of the event organizers who was helping me moderate said, "Did you see that Zoom-bomb comment?! I'm so sorry about that." I hadn't seen it at all, but she filled me in. An unregistered individual had logged into the event and dropped into the group chat, "This is Communist propaganda!" and followed it with a Bible verse.

Such comments are part of the reality of being a vocal antiracist. But here is what stung: Only two people at the event replied to the comment. As I was literally telling 500 people that key attributes of being an accomplice are opting in and taking action, only two people did anything when faced with a very specific moment to opt in and take action. The other 498—including the organizers—did nothing. A few days later, the organizers did call to apologize for what had happened and let me know that some attendees had sent screenshots of the Zoom-bomb and complained about the aggressor's behavior. I was, of course, open to the conversation, but it didn't escape me that all of the people who showed up after the fact to rehash the incident and agree that it shouldn't have happened did nothing *in the moment* to address the person who actually needed intervention. I personally don't need to be told that it was unacceptable. But that Zoom-bomber sure needs to know—and an accomplice would have told them.

Every day has moments like this. Moments when you can do one thing to show up on behalf of another person. Moments to speak up and have someone's back when they aren't sure they can do it for themselves (and shouldn't have to). Moments when you can course-correct an inappropriate person or an out-of-line comment. You can do that with your truth and in your way. Someone in my presentation could have typed, "I'm really enjoying the session!" Someone else could have added, "This has nothing to do with communism." And others could have added their personal opinion about what they were learning. No one needed to shame the original commenter or start a fight. What I needed, and what BIPOC at work need, is for the people who claim to support us to drown out and out-number the other voices. If fifty people had posted positive and supportive comments, the Zoom-bomber might have started to reconsider their position or at least understood that there was a better way to engage in productive discussion (there was a Q&A, after all). Looking back to my past workplaces, had only one person spoken up on my behalf or addressed the microaggressions, I might have had a very different experience and a very different career trajectory (though I am very happy with where I ended up).

All we know about people at the end of the day is how they behave. You can say one thing and behave differently—we have all witnessed that at some point in our lives. Behavior is what people see, feel, and believe. We don't need statements from companies about Black Lives Matter; we need action. We need to see what they are doing to extend that sentiment into changed circumstances. An accomplice prepares for moments to support others. We all know these moments will happen at some point, so rehearse, record your retorts, and plan on being the person who steps up.

ACCOMPLICESHIP IS SELF-WORK

As awareness and pressure have grown around the issues of race and inequity in the workplace, so too have services to help organizations deal with the issues that plague them. Some DEIAA professionals will go into a company and help leaders set goals, create employee resource groups or affinity groups, and review processes to assess biases. Setting quantifiable goals is usually a go-to impulse for leaders and managers when starting DEIAA work. I see it all the time. They list the number of people they'd like to hire, the pipelines they want to build, or maybe the programs they want to have in place to support BIPOC employees. Yet, when I look at those outcomes, it feels very uncreative. Is that as visionary as we can get when it comes to the experiences we are creating in our workplaces? Is a quota the best we can aim for?

When I assess what needs to be addressed at most companies, it's not policies, programs, or procedures. I start with the people and the culture those people create. When it comes to workplaces, individuals make up teams and teams make up organizations. For any change to happen at the organizational level, it also has to happen at the individual level.

Who we are *at* work starts with who we are *outside* of work. We have to disavow the notion that we have multiple selves: a work self and a personal self. We have one self, and that whole self needs to commit to the work that being an accomplice requires. We're conditioned to split ourselves into pieces—we're "work Jenny" and "mom Jenny" and "out-with-friends Jenny" and "at-church Jenny." Yet, this journey from ally to accomplice has to be about you as a whole person. Splitting ourselves into pieces just makes us feel triply and quadruply responsible for taking action as an accomplice in all those situations and circumstances. If "work Jenny" and "mom Jenny" each have to create more equitable environments, it doubles the perception of the effort required. And that perception—albeit inaccurate—is one of the biggest reasons people opt out of the work: it feels like extra work. Being an accomplice is not like a hobby or a skill you're learning over on the side; it's a practice you embed into your everyday way of life. It's simply leaving your house and infusing the tenets of equitable and just practices into how you live your daily life. I tell folks there's no way to put on an inclusion blazer and wear that blazer while you work, then take it off and hang it up when you are done working. That's not what this is. It's about a whole lifestyle change.

Individuals have a big role in creating welcoming and inclusive environments at work. It goes back to the point we just covered: Teams and workplaces are made of individuals—their actions and behaviors. If you hire ten BIPOC into an unwelcoming culture, one that was not created with them in mind or that only cares that ten BIPOC bodies show up every day to achieve the "diversity" success metric, you won't have ten BIPOC employees in a year. One or two may stick around, but most will move on because they won't thrive or succeed if the shared definition of diversity is simply 15 percent BIPOC on staff. Diversity mandates and board quotas can't change the behavior individuals exhibit every day at the coffee maker or in meetings. Hiring three more Black people won't make the established employees feel responsible for creating a welcoming environment for the new hires.

Last year I met with a leadership team of an international company at the beginning of our coaching engagement. No matter how I engage with a client, one of the first discussions is about their goals. I ask them what they want to achieve and what outcomes they want for their DEIAA work. Like most teams, these executives had specific ideas of what diversity would look like at their organization. For example, the CEO had a very detailed understanding of the data around their pipeline and how many BIPOC needed to be in it to ensure enough some made it into the final round of applicants. They knew they wanted to hit those numbers—and they believed diversity would come if they hit those numbers. We had a lively conversation, and I gave them several goals to aim for as we embarked on our work. In the next session we started doing the personal work to reach those goals. We asked the team: *What are your greatest DEIAA challenges as a leader? How do those challenges impact your leadership? Do you feel like you have everything you need to lead at this moment? If not, what support do you need? How can we help you better understand DEIAA as it relates to your leadership?* Question after question, the team was silent or the exchanges were stilted. They didn't—or couldn't—engage when it came to actually talking about race, racial identity, and their own role and capabilities as leaders. Very different from when we were discussing diversity goals and quotas.

That experience (and many previous ones) is exactly why I

prioritize personal DEIAA work before organizational DEIAA work. If we don't address the personal side of what individuals bring into workplaces, teams will never get more comfortable with the necessary topics or improve their ability to have conversations about race as fluidly as they can talk about goals. That group of executives oversees everything at their global organization: They lead the teams and people, set the company priorities and goals, and drive the work culture. And they do so while being wholly uncomfortable with race. Imagine that team hiring a BIPOC into the space and culture they created and maintain (consciously or not). How welcoming would it feel for BIPOC if their colleagues couldn't talk about or acknowledge race, which is such an integral part of their identity? No matter how hard that leadership team worked on their pipeline, they wouldn't make a dent in how their workplace feels for incoming BIPOC or create equitable conditions unless they got more comfortable with race on a personal level.

Creating an inclusive workplace is self-work. Yes, you may be doing it to enhance your success at work or improve your DEIAA numbers, but you will succeed only if you embark on a personal journey to understand yourself in relation to race, history, and accountability. In the coming pages I will share stories and data that aren't about work or workplaces. Race, racialized experiences, and racism don't start or stop at the office door. All people bring their personal experiences into work situations, and it's crucial that leaders consider that when making inclusive spaces. Nothing is just about work—we are all people who exist in a sometimes-terrifying world, and whatever happens to us remains with us as we move through the workplace. As a person, you carry such things too. You bring those experiences with you. You bring an accumulation of personal and professional interactions, relationships, and knowledge to everything you do. If you're white, you bring a privilege that you might not (yet) be aware of into every space you enter. You bring your *whole self*. And if we're going to make spaces for individuals with all different types of experiences to come to our workplaces with all of who they are, we must think of accompliceship work as more than just a leadership skill—it's a personal practice.

Truthfully, a series of awakenings, discoveries, lessons, and setbacks often happen before the average leader steps fully into being an accomplice at work. If you are a fifty-year-old CEO and you're beginning this work for the first time in earnest, you might feel frustrated. Consider this: you've been working in your industry or profession for decades, and you likely consider yourself an expert at parts of your job. But most people are only infants, at best, when it comes to antiracism, which leads to lots of first steps and scraped knees. If your lived experience is as a white person, your day-to-day existence hasn't primed you for antiracism work because you're rarely confronted with oppression or barriers due to your race. That's one of the frustrating aspects of this work for accomplished people—it's learning a new way of thinking and behaving at a point in our lives when our thoughts and behaviors are pretty established. But I assure you, it is possible to move through the frustration and develop a fierce accomplice mindset. Imagine this for your future self:

- You have a cogent understanding of the concepts of race, racism, and racialization.

- You are aware of the historical, political, and social implications of your race and other races.

- You are comfortable having conversations about and making decisions based on race.

- You are more confident in asking questions that will lead you through an antiracist process.

- You are familiar with strategies to expand your lived experience and engage with the differences around you.

If you've said to yourself, "I'm going to commit to being antiracist, and I'm going to do the necessary work to make my environment more equitable," this book will help you figure out how to put that commitment into practice in your life and business. It will share what you need to understand and do to never miss an opportunity to be the best version of yourself. In any given situation, you will be able to ask, "What would an accomplice do?" and have a path forward to find your answer.

I hear from people all the time, "What should I do? What can I do?" My answer: You must develop a practice that you can use to answer those questions for yourself in any given situation. I can't give you scripts or walk you through every type of conversation you will have around race or BIPOC feedback about your work culture—I wouldn't be able to do that justice because each circumstance requires something very specific to it and to you. But I can provide a new way for you to frame your approach to race and DEIAA work. It's like the teaching-a-person-to-fish allegory—I can do more and you can go further if I show you how to find many answers rather than handing you just one.

Learning a practice, rather than a checklist or set of specific actions, will serve you, and everyone who wants to make change, best. A practice is made up of the actions, rituals, and activities that help you develop a proficiency in something. This book provides advice and knowledge for beginning your practice, but as every teacher knows, there is no way to share *everything*. I hope to teach you how to think differently about diversity and inclusion work in order to act effectively in your situation—because what we've been doing isn't working. A practice, while it might sound passive, is actually pretty darn active! If you commit to daily work and engagement, you will make progress and observe real change. That's what accompliceship is about. It is the actions, rituals, and activities you do to practice an antiracist way of living and leading. This is antiracism in action.

THE THREE As

A practice is never done or fully achieved. You may become really good at it, but there will always be opportunities to improve, learn more, or refine your behaviors. And, as we know from other things we practice, each day is new. You might be great at something one day and the next you might suck or struggle. That is all part and parcel of a practice.

On your journey you will always be learning new things. At times you will seek out new information intentionally, as in research, and at other times it will come at you unexpectedly, perhaps in the form of feedback. Either way, an accomplice does something with the new information. It can be easy to read about new ideas and absorb new concepts without changing anything. What we really need to do is change how we *are* based on the new information. An accomplice is always working to grow and adapt to the world around them.

The Three As are *awareness*, *analysis*, and *action*. You can bring these to every situation to engage more fully and cement your learning.

I often describe this tool with a set of questions:
- Awareness: What do I know now that I didn't know before?
- Analysis: What do I need to learn?
- Action: How do I do something with this information?

Awareness is the cornerstone to being an accomplice. Awareness happens on two levels: self-awareness and social-historical awareness. Both aspects bring so much to every moment and every experience we have with other people, even when we're not thinking about them (perhaps more so when we aren't thinking about them). We cannot do any good in any space without a high degree of self-awareness *and* an awareness of how we all got to the place we are now. Turning the mirror on yourself is truly the starting place for everything. An honest understanding of what you see in the mirror and how you contribute to the world around you is always ground zero.

Once you're aware of something, you can't become unaware of it. That's when deepening your analysis kicks in. And so you ask, "what do I need to learn now?" Once we're aware of the things we don't know or know only a little about, we can learn more and think critically about how to expand our knowledge. That leads to greater self-awareness and more context for everything around us. Only then can we move to action.

Taking action is what we need. It is easy to learn things and to feel knowledgeable, but moving to action makes the impact. Yet, it's the hardest part. It raises your blood pressure because it's scary. Doing something beyond talking about how crappy a situation is hard, I know that.

But you need all three As to make change. Awareness and analysis without action keep you on the sidelines of change, where allies often remain. Action without awareness and analysis can be dangerous because the actions can hurt and offend people or derail efforts entirely. Used together, this powerful combination begins with an inward focus, on your personal perspective, and moves outward so you can be useful to others. The Three As allow you to apply your learning to yourself and to your immediate situation and ensure you're opting in with a level of consistency—all of which will supplement and complement your antiracist practice. Without them, you might go around picking up bits and pieces of information and putting them into a little mental basket rather than applying them to your life. The Three As will help you change how you think *and* what you do.

At the end of each chapter, I will present two sets of information to help you explore the cycle of awareness, analysis, and action. In the Pause for Awareness and Analysis sections I provide questions to guide introspection on your daily practice as a leader and colleague. In the Move to Action sections I provide actions you can take on that chapter's topics to enhance or deepen your practice. The actions I suggest are not everything you can and should do; they simply provide a starting place for engaging in an ongoing practice. How you choose to move to action should be connected to your own awareness, analysis, and environment. Together, I hope the sections help you answer the three questions of the cycle: What do I know, what do I need to learn, and what am I going to do?

With all that said, I also want to add that this work—this antiracist practice that requires action—is not as hard as you might think. If you're daunted by it, take it slowly. If you're a little afraid, spend time with your feelings—and then move to action. With myself and with clients, I have found that when we want something and care enough about the possibilities and opportunities on the other side of our efforts, it won't feel like a lot of work. We do things we care about. Imagine applying for a job you really want and landing an interview. What would you do? You would research the heck out of the company or organization. You would read every word on their website—from the mission, vision, and values to the leadership bios. You would look up recent press coverage and the current stock price and its history. You would research the board of directors and the events that the company hosts. You would brainstorm interview questions and compose responses to prepare you for any possible topic. If you're super savvy and it's a nonprofit organization, you might look up the Guidestar report to know what the top salaries are and how much of a salary you can negotiate for. The effort you put into this wouldn't feel like work—it would feel like learning, growing, expanding, and preparing—because you want it and care about it. If you want to be an accomplice, the path to leading teams and being a fierce accomplice will feel the same way—like learning, growing, and expanding.

Everything you need to be an accomplice is already within you. Like Neo in *The Matrix*, you'll find there is no external magic. You are competent and capable; this is like learning anything new—though it might challenge you more than some topics—but you can do it. You just have to *do* it. That's the work.

PART 1: WHAT YOU NEED TO KNOW TO DEVELOP YOUR PRACTICE

To engage in any practice, you must first learn information that helps you understand the context of the work you will be doing. As it pertains to an antiracist practice in particular, jumping into action without a solid foundation of understanding causes harm. It's why leaders' efforts aren't effective and they make so many mistakes—because they don't truly understand the broader issues, history, circumstances, and people they are working on and with.

Part 1 will help you increase your understanding around the topics of race so you can engage in action from a more informed starting point. When you have more context, you will have more awareness and be better equipped to observe situations and circumstances with an eye toward inequity and injustice.

What You Need to Know
The origins of race and racism
Defining truth: Race, a made-up construct, and racism, the power hierarchy assigned to race, are our oldest and most persistent problems and still impact us today.

White supremacy culture is always at play
Defining truth: White supremacy culture has permeated our culture and needs to be undone before inclusion can take root.

Privilege and power are our paths to impact
Defining truth: Privilege is the unearned access you possess; power is the action you take with that access.

CHAPTER 2: THE ORIGINS AND IMPACT OF RACE AND RACISM

You Can't Dismantle What You Don't Understand

I'd like to introduce you to Kathy, one of The Woke Coach's clients. When she was hired as CEO of a one-hundred-person B2B company, one of her strategic priorities was DEIAA (a priority she defined herself!). Yet, seven years later, here we were in our new-client discussion, and when I asked about what efforts they had made in the DEIAA space, she and her fifteen-person leadership team were very transparent about where they were in their DEIAA journey: stuck. I could tell she was frustrated that she had made no strides toward her self-proclaimed priority. She told us, "I don't really know all the things I need to know, but what I do know is that we're not doing a good enough job. It's something we talk about at leadership meetings, but nothing ever gets done." This scenario is all too common at organizations.

While talking about diversity and inclusion is the beginning of the work, language only, with no behavioral changes, won't produce new outcomes—and you'll get stuck. Kathy was like many of the CEOs and executives we meet: excellent and smart at their core job, but very green when it came to being an accomplice in a workplace.

That inexperience is understandable. DEIAA has not been a valued area of expertise for most companies until recently, and because she is white, her lived experience didn't prepare her.

To help Kathy and her team take real steps toward their DEIAA strategic priority, we sent The Woke Coach temperature check survey to everyone in the organization to assess the culture. These extensive surveys are our way of learning more about the people, internal dynamics, and opinions within the organization—aside from and in addition to what the leadership team has already shared with us. We specifically ask about DEIAA efforts and the employees' experience with race and racial identity as well as overall work culture assessment questions. For example, we ask, "What is going well and what could be improved as it relates to DEIAA at this company?" While this seems like a very basic question, most company surveys do not ask about diversity and inclusion, even though it is exactly what we must know to make progress.

Fast forward a few weeks to Kathy, the head of Human Resources, and me sitting in a large conference room on a Tuesday morning. They were anxiously paging through The Woke Coach report based on the results from the survey. Presenting our observations and assessments of survey results always begins an anxious conversation because leaders feel like they aren't in control. Our clients, often for the first time, realize that they're at the mercy of a third party—us—to give them information about their own company. We wrote the questions, and the employees responded to us (not to anyone at the organization), so Kathy had no idea how it was going to all turn out. Leaders often start questioning things during this time: *Do people actually like it here? What will they say about me and our work culture? Have the staff been hiding things from me?*

I know how Kathy is feeling at this moment. You might know how Kathy is feeling too—maybe you've felt or still feel this way. This vulnerable moment is a necessary step for this work if you're a white person. When it comes to the overall success of an organization, leaders and managers may rely on what they know to be true about their industry and lived experience to create the conditions for and ultimately achieve success—and it usually works. However, as it relates to DEIAA, those same leaders often have deficiencies in their lived experience or knowledge, so creating an environment primed for success is more challenging.

Kathy had no idea what to expect, and I could tell she was incredibly uncomfortable. What we find over and over again is that employees withhold experiences and opinions from leadership but will share everything if given a trustworthy opportunity. When asked directly about their impressions of DEIAA efforts or racism in the workplace, they'll be very honest about what's going on and often even provide solutions. Kathy's employees were no different. She paged through the feedback and spent a good deal of time reading excerpts from what people had shared. I could tell she was absorbing it very earnestly and trying to process all of the new information in real time. In the Organizational Culture survey category, responses showed that BIPOC at Kathy's company reported receiving poor treatment, experiencing microaggressions, and witnessing racist practices, and they shared that there was a lack of trust and respect for each other (their words were *hierarchical*, *siloed*, and *old fashioned*). Direct quotes included "Some of the white employees are resistant to change or think that we are just doing [DEIAA] to 'check a box' instead of truly investing in it" and "The management team could benefit from some training on racial microaggressions in the workplace." Kathy's face fell. She hired us because she deeply wanted to engage in meaningful DEIAA work (finally), and learning what was happening among her staff and the depth of people's experiences and opinions revealed a lot about how far behind they were as a company. Saddened and shocked at the results, she responded, with a defeated and slightly defensive sigh, "I haven't seen racism here." I asked, "How would you have seen it? Do you know what to look for?"

Not surprisingly, the gap between what leaders say about their organization and what our survey results tell us can be vast. In this case, the unfiltered responses challenged what Kathy thought she knew about her company. She had been making decisions and setting goals believing she knew what was happening inside her organization. As an engaged leader, she thought she had access to the full set of circumstances her colleagues experienced. The survey feedback showed her that she didn't actually have the knowledge or access she believed she'd had this whole time. At that moment, she learned that her workplace was toxic. And right on the heels of reading about the toxicity, she realized she'd had no idea it was happening or that people were experiencing such harm under her leadership. As a white person, she wasn't going to be privy to the racism that was unfolding around her. All of a sudden, it became clear to her that she didn't know what she thought she knew, and also that there was a lot more she had to learn. Kathy knew her company had some problems already, which is why she hired The Woke Coach, and yet the survey showed her she had even bigger problems than expected. She thought she had hired me to learn how to do DEIAA; now she knew that she needed to learn about her own organization and the people within it before any DEIAA work could begin.

If you, too, are a leader who doesn't understand racism and the various forms it takes, you might also be sad or shocked to hear from people at your company that racism exists in your workplace. Often, people feel that it's not happening because they can't see it. But if you're a white leader, you won't have access to most racist exchanges or interactions because only those that are huge and egregious are within your purview.

Hearing Kathy's comment about not seeing racism is hard, even though I hear it often. It speaks to the trauma I have from places and spaces that didn't support me and leaders who didn't "see" racism in situations that were definitely rooted in assumptions and biases about race, and my racial identity in particular. Imagine telling people something is there but no one believes you because they don't see it. Imagine having to bring it up over and over again in an attempt to make things better. What Kathy learned is that racism isn't always blatant discrimination or individuals yelling slurs. If you're only looking for racism like that, you likely won't see all the other ways it's showing up and will continue to allow harm in your workplace.

If you're here to take your antiracism work more seriously and fully apply it at work, you've likely educated yourself somewhat about some of our current issues. However, an even deeper understanding of how race came to be defined and weaponized is crucial for accompliceship. Knowing the history and basics of the concept will chip away at some of the fear that you, like most people, bring to situations. Understanding the language and concepts is a great starting point for the "what if I mess up?" question that keeps many people from engaging in conversations about race and racism. You will be less likely to mess up egregiously if you know the facts, are familiar with the terminology and use it accurately, and can ask questions from an educated perspective.

In client conversation after client conversation, I've also observed that many white leaders haven't spent deep personal time discussing or reflecting on race—what race is, the history of race, or where these labels came from and why and how they inequitably unfold in deeply traumatic circumstances. I detect this when people say, "We have a color-blind culture" and still hire The Woke Coach: they know they're not where they should be with diversity and inclusion. Sometimes I ask clients directly about how their race impacts their leadership and many say, "We're all just part of the human race," or mention people of color in their lives (an adopted child, a Black husband, an Asian friend) as evidence that they aren't unaware of racialized circumstances. Occasionally a few are very honest and reply, "I've never thought about my race as a leader, specifically." If I push past the personal question and ask for data that demonstrates the depth of racism in their industry, they squirm a little because they don't know the data or have even written it off with comments like, "It's a pipeline issue," or, "This is just a really white industry." Each of these reactions, in all their overt and covert forms, displays how far leaders can get in their company and career without ever considering race. Meanwhile, race is not the only thing BIPOC want to talk about—we would rather come to work and talk about work, about contributing, collaborating, and succeeding together—but often we have to talk about race because others don't understand it.

Finally, I have discovered that many people's formal education about race and racism started and ended in high school. They learned about slavery and some version of the civil rights movement but not much more. The effects of racism extend far before and beyond not being allowed to sit at the front of the bus. Here we are, at a time when race and racism are a significant part of our cultural conversation, and if your history lesson stopped in high school (or you've listened to a few podcasts or watched some documentaries since George Floyd was murdered), you don't have much information, lived experience, or historical context to draw on for effective conversations with BIPOC peers and staff, to draft practices and policies with equity in mind, or to engage in meaningful change.

SO, LET'S TALK ABOUT RACE

You might have wondered, *Isn't ethnicity the same as race? What's the difference?* You might have thought, *I've never spit on someone because of their race or harmed someone intentionally; how can I be racist?* Racism doesn't just show up as Klan members storming in the front door; it's (hopefully) subtler than that. How might it show up? You might see (and, quite frankly, might commit yourself) racial microaggressions, which are smaller yet still very harmful comments and behaviors rooted in biases or a lack of awareness. Microaggressions are micro: They aren't always obvious to anyone other than the offended person. For example, BIPOC tell me that people within their own company assume that they're not in leadership roles. Sure, one could say, "Well, that's an honest mistake." But when it happens repeatedly, we know something is going on. You might see systems and structures that benefit white people to the detriment of everyone else, like HR processes at Fortune 500 companies that disproportionately discriminate against Black and brown applicants based on their names.[13] You might observe an unspoken but very common habit of hiring people that will "fit in," that is, who are like everyone else at the company. If you don't have a thorough understanding of race, it's difficult to detect racism and its many forms in the many facets of our daily lives. So, we see well-meaning white folks trying to fight something they don't understand because they have not closely examined it. It's very hard to dismantle racist systems and structures if you don't even know what you're trying to fight.

To be the best accomplice ever, you need to understand three critical facets of race and racism:

- What race and racism really are

- The types of racism that unfold in the real world in layered and often invisible ways

- How racism impacts all of us every day

This is, of course, not everything there is to know about race and racism, but these points are the bare minimum you need to know to take action in ways that are useful, meaningful, and self-aware. And they are the bare minimum you need to know to fully engage with the rest of the book.

---

[13] Kline, Patrick, Evan K. Rose, and Christopher R. Walters. 2022. "Systemic Discrimination Among Large U.S. Employers." *The Quarterly Journal of Economics* 137, no. 4 (June): 1963–2036. https://academic.oup.com/qje/article/137/4/1963/6605934.

TO LEAD TEAMS AS AN ACCOMPLICE, YOU DON'T HAVE TO SEE RACE IN ABSOLUTELY EVERYTHING, BUT YOU DO HAVE TO ACKNOWLEDGE THAT RACE CAN AFFECT ANY GIVEN SITUATION OR CIRCUMSTANCE.

You have to be willing to ask what you might not know and what you might need to learn to proceed into or through a situation. You personally don't have to recognize racism in every form and in every moment. Your goal, instead, is to assume you don't have all the information about a given circumstance and to seek out perspectives and people who can help you think beyond your lived experiences. Your role as a leader then shifts from believing or hoping you know everything to pursuing whatever information you lack (and there will always be some—we all have limitations!).

One of my clients came to me recently from this very position: He knew his company was trying to attract and hire more BIPOC, and he also knew that they hadn't been successful at it before. It had become clear to him what information he needed to proceed as accomplice: inclusive hiring practices. Rather than keep trying what wasn't working, he humbly asked, "We know we need to change, so how do we do better?" He allowed what he *didn't* know to guide his leadership as much as what he did know.

Businesses and leaders today must deal with race and racism whether they were planning to or not. Take the egregious, restrictive voting laws enacted in Georgia in the spring of 2021. Customers pressured companies with headquarters or large presences in Georgia to speak up. Delta, Major League Baseball, and Coca-Cola, and other companies had customers and employees who wanted to know—in some cases demanded to know—where the businesses stood on the issue because it was important to their consumer decisions. The leaders of those companies had to go on record with their statements. Imagine how having a deepened awareness of history, race, and the lived realities of people impacted by that law could assist a leader in those moments. With that, leaders would be better equipped to address complex histories and current events with an awareness that would give them, and their companies, credibility and authenticity. It would create the possibility of contributing to the conversation, not just responding to legislation about it.

What Is Race?

The National Museum of African American History and Culture offers this definition:

> "The notion of race is a social construct designed to divide people into groups ranked as superior and inferior. The scientific consensus is that race, in this sense, has no biological basis—we are all one race, the human race. Racial identity, however, is very real. And, in a racialized society like the United States, everyone is assigned a racial identity whether they are aware of it or not."

As an accomplice, here is what you need to understand from that definition:

Race is a social construct designed to divide people into groups ranked as superior and inferior. This important point is perhaps one of the least understood. Humans invented race. It is not rooted in anything other than our minds, mindsets, and history. Many things around us are socially constructed, such as currency and marriage. This alone does not make race good or bad, real or not real, but it's essential to know that it is a concept created by people to order the world. Socially constructed categories have social, economic, and political implications but no basis in biology. DNA may help determine ethnicity, but that is distinct from race; that is how people of Nordic descent may all be considered white and people of sub-Saharan descent may all be considered Black, and yet they can have very different ethnic backgrounds.

The concept of race was created intentionally as a means of giving power to those who have, over time, become classified as white. Through the years, whiteness has evolved to include some people, like Irish, Italian, and Jewish immigrants, and yet always excludes other people, like South American and African immigrants. The fact that race has evolved underscores that it was created as a tool to be wielded by people in positions of power. When it was convenient, some lighter-skinned people were allowed into the white space. Racial categories have always been fluid and reorganized. Over time, even the racial categories in the US census have changed.[14] And up until 1960, census takers decided the race of the person they were counting; it was not self-identified.

The scientific consensus is that race, in this sense, has no biological basis. At a biological level, two Black people are no more like each other than a white and Black person are like each other. There is no DNA marker for race. DNA can tell you where your ancestors likely came from, and DNA controls your physical appearance, but that information does not accurately predict your race.[15]

In a racialized society like the United States, everyone is assigned a racial identity.
The color of our skin is a defining attribute that others see or

---

[14] Anna Brown, "The Changing Categories the U.S. Census Has Used to Measure Race," February, 25, 2020, https://www.pewresearch.org/fact-tank/2020/02/25/the-changing-categories-the-u-s-has-used-to-measure-race/.

[15] Jack Herrera, "DNA Tests Can't Tell You Your Race," Popular Science, April 26, 2021, https://www.popsci.com/story/science/dna-tests-myth-ancestry-race/.

encounter before anything else. When they see it, they associate that skin color with a particular race (or combinations of races). The way others categorize our race determines how we're perceived and treated and shapes how our bodies are governed. The result is that likeness is found in how people are racialized and treated. When we talk about the Black or brown lived experience, there are similarities but they're not rooted in bodies. They're rooted in how society categorizes those bodies and treats them according to those categorizations. A racialized experience can happen even though race is a human invention.

Continually seeking a deeper understanding of US history and race relations might seem like a lot, but it truly is the key to engaging in accomplice behaviors. Think of going deep on race like this: A business would never roll out an initiative or launch a new product without doing market research. The importance of understanding who you're trying to connect to and with is something we learn very early on in business strategy. If you're a leader, it's likewise imperative to understand the people around you and the people you want to attract to the company.

People, and their successes, are your primary "product" as a leader. If you're leading diverse or relatively diverse teams, it's important to know each employee's experience in your culture and what they need to bring their best work to projects. Asking for direct and honest feedback about how to improve the current conditions will show you exactly what needs are being addressed or ignored. As I mentioned previously, the most common comment I hear from BIPOC is that they can't bring their whole selves to work. Ask your employees what they might be leaving at home and what would make the workplace more welcoming for those leave-behinds. This is a simple way to deepen analysis of your current user needs. If you are leading all-white teams right now but want to attract people of color to work at your company, you have to understand what new hires need. You can't just "go to market" with a job description and hope that BIPOC or members of other groups underrepresented at your company will apply. By examining your internal culture before attracting people who are not already part of it, you can identify what changes must be made to make the company a welcoming place that feels inclusive for new folks.

Similarly, I bet as a leader you have a thorough understanding of your industry's history, where it is right now, and where it's going. You read industry press, news, and books about your niche, and you attend lectures or conferences to learn what's on the horizon. You have to do the same as an accomplice. You can't be an effective accomplice if you don't understand how we got here, where we are right now, and where we need to be. If you are out in the world trying to be an accomplice without understanding what you're working against or for—if you've rushed into doing something just for the sake of doing something—your product, like any that fails to meet users' needs, won't be successful.

To be an accomplice who leads or manages inclusive teams, you have to believe that the long and complicated history of race informs individuals and our circumstances today. I witness a lot of people trying to engage in DEIAA efforts without doing a deep dive into the history and realities of race because they're anxious and just want to get to the solution. How might you determine that you're rushing toward a solution without doing deeper work? It looks like this:

- You haven't budgeted for the work.

- You haven't thought about what you want to do differently or what outcomes would be meaningful to your organization.

- When selecting a partner to assist you and your company on DEIAA work, you are most interested in prices, not the education, training, or coaching that will be included.

- You make someone else responsible for the work.

- You believe that if an individual or a singular department is doing the work, it will take root with you, the executives, and the rest of the organization.

These are indicators that the slow, deepening part of the work is not being well considered. While it's not a terrible thing to be overly focused on reaching a solution, it means you haven't taken the time to fully understand the issues and may not be planning on taking the appropriate amount of time.

RACISM

I like definitions. I believe it's incredibly important to be very specific with words and their meanings because people have different definitions, especially of controversial words like *racism*, *diversity*, and *equity*. [Pro tip: Always get specific and define the words used in your DEIAA work; it cuts through a lot of misunderstanding.] Here's my working definition of *racism*.

> Racism is a system of oppression that consists of racial prejudice and discrimination—supported by institutional power and authority—used to the advantage of one race and the disadvantage of another race or races. The critical element which differentiates racism from prejudice and discrimination is the use of institutional power and authority to support white supremacy, reiterate prejudices, and enforce discriminatory behaviors in systemic ways with far-reaching outcomes and effects.

It's a system of oppression. Racism is not just one behavior or situation. There are multiple types, each of which has its own roots and effects. We'll get into those types next.

It consists of racial prejudice and discrimination—supported by institutional power and authority . . . This is where I unequivocally announce: There is no "reverse racism." There is no such thing because racism must be supported by institutional power and authority, and I'm here to tell you that BIPOC don't have that. Systems are in place that support where and how power is currently held (in whiteness) and that keep power located with certain individuals (those who are white identified). Individuals may have racial biases and prejudices, but those are distinct from racism. Prejudice without power impacts individuals. Prejudice coupled with power—that is, racism—results in discrimination, oppression, and racialization of entire groups as well as individuals.

. . . used to the advantage of one race and the disadvantage of another race or races. The construct of race is a hierarchy, never an even playing field. As it has played out historically, race requires some groups to be superior and some to be inferior. But because racism is based on something that is socially constructed, it can be socially deconstructed. It's not out of our hands. We created it, and we can control it. I can't change my skin color, but how we categorize or place value on my skin color can change.

Use of institutional power and authority to support white supremacy, reiterate prejudices, and enforce discriminatory behaviors . . . Racism upholds and supports whiteness at all costs. It's purely a tool to perpetuate whiteness as the superior identity, even when white people are not the global or national majority.

. . . with far-reaching outcomes and effects. Like those location-based apps constantly running on your phone, racism is operating in the background whether we know it or not. Unless it's turned off, it just churns away while your attention is elsewhere. And that's the brilliance of racism: It's been so ingrained into our culture that we don't have to do anything to perpetuate it: it just continues. The effects are not bound by time or industry or generation, and thus they're complex and intertwined. As we get into the types of racism below, the complexity and interconnectedness will become more obvious.

One important aspect of my work is illuminating the *types* of racism for leaders because many consider racism to be one-on-one and explicit expressions of hate or bigotry. But racism is so much more than solitary acts, and the most common forms of racism are much subtler than most people think. To help make sense of that, I cover four types of racism most frequently in my work: interpersonal, institutional, structural, and internalized. Other types exist, and some forms have different names, but these four types will give you insight into some of the ways racism manifests in daily life.

Interpersonal Racism

Interpersonal racism occurs between individuals. It's the holding of negative attitudes toward a different race or culture. When a white person takes their misinformation and stereotypes about another group and performs an act of harassment, exclusion, marginalization, discrimination, hate, or violence, they commit an act of interpersonal racism toward an individual or group.

When we move beyond talking about prejudice and stereotypes in our society, we generally focus on acts of interpersonal racism. These are the acts we hear about in the media—a hate crime, a specific instance of job or housing discrimination, a celebrity's negative racial comments about BIPOC, racial profiling, or violence by a police officer toward BIPOC. This is the type of racism that white people focus on when denying that they're racist.

These acts are definitely damaging. But the system of racism is much larger, and racism would not be eliminated by ending these personal acts. One way our culture keeps racism in place is by focusing only on individual acts of racism and the "rotten apples." If we're thinking about those acts of racism as individual bad applcs, we will spend less time understanding and addressing the pervasiveness of the systems that also harm BIPOC. If people keep saying "I'm not racist" and thinking that means racism doesn't exist, we'll never solve the deeper, more complex issues.

Institutional Racism

Institutional racism refers to organizational and cultural practices that perpetuate racial inequity, in which the benefits are structured to advantage powerful groups at the expense of others. Jim Crow laws and redlining practices are two examples of institutional racism.

Institutional racism operates through the policies, procedures, and practices of particular institutions in our society. Racism is built into the healthcare system, the education system, the employment market, the housing market, the media, and the criminal justice system, just to name a few. In all of these institutions, racism operates within and throughout the system, without the need for individual racist acts. Following the rules or norms of the system produces outcomes that benefit white people and harm BIPOC because the rules and norms are set up to reproduce racism. For example, during most of this country's history, it was illegal for white and Black people to marry across racial lines, eat together in public, travel together, or shop together. The shopkeepers, bus and train conductors, public officials who enforced segregation weren't necessarily participating in interpersonal racism—they were just law-abiding white citizens.

Similarly, a white schoolteacher can teach her students equally, address each student's needs, and help everyone advance to the next grade level. But, if she is teaching in a school or school system where there are no BIPOC students, where white students are tracked into higher-level courses than Black students, where BIPOC students are disciplined more harshly than white students, or where the curriculum does not reflect the contributions of BIPOC to our society, then the teacher is perpetuating institutional racism despite any "color-blind" efforts.

Structural Racism (a.k.a. Systemic Racism)

Structural racism refers to the ways in which the joint operation of institutions (i.e., inter-institutional arrangements and interactions) produces racialized outcomes, even in the absence of racist intent. Indicators of structural racism include power inequalities, unequal access to opportunities, and differing policy outcomes by race. Because these effects are created and reinforced across multiple institutions, the root causes of structural racism are difficult to isolate.

One example is the school-to-prison pipeline in which BIPOC children are pushed out of our schools and into the criminal legal system. In this example, racism within the school system, the welfare system, child protective services, the foster-care system, and the criminal legal system interacts to produce an outcome that disproportionately limits the educational opportunities of young BIPOC and disproportionately disciplines and locks them up. Another example is how lack of affordable health care and access to affordable healthy food options, in concert with higher exposure to toxic chemicals and other forms of pollution, employment discrimination, and housing segregation produces greater health problems, shorter life spans, lower wages, and greater levels of poverty for BIPOC communities.

The cumulative impact of interpersonal, institutional, and cultural racism within our society creates a system of structural racism. This complex and interconnected system has far-reaching outcomes and effects. The different types of racism overlap, reinforce, and amplify the different treatment that BIPOC receive compared to that which white people receive, ensuring different life outcomes. Structural racism is cumulative, pervasive, and durable. That is both the brilliance and deep harm of structural racism: it masks as "just the way things are" so that inequitable outcomes appear natural as well.

Internalized Racism

Internalized racism is a racist belief that you've chosen to make part of who you are, regardless of whether you act on it or not. For some BIPOC it shows up as internalized racial oppression; for whites and some individuals who are not Black it shows up as internalized racial superiority.

If you're white, it's just racism, like Archie Bunker and the people in the robes and hoods. It's the belief that others are less than, held in order to feel better than. If you have internalized racism, you don't see yourself as separate from the core tenets of racist thought.

For BIPOC it comes out as internalized racial oppression, which looks like judging other BIPOC for not fitting into white culture, assimilating with dominant culture and believing that distinguishes them from others in a superior way, and hating the parts of themselves that don't fit into the dominant culture, that is, whiteness. Internalized racism is closely related to interpersonal racism, but interpersonal racism is when we let our internalized beliefs direct our external interactions.

If you have a basic understanding of the history and systems integral to race and racism and how they play out in your industry and community, you can better interact with and be of service to people impacted by that history and those systems. Deepening your understanding of the nuances of race and racism will help you notice less obvious effects of racism in your day-to-day world, such as why you have few Black neighbors (or none) or why public schools in lower-income neighborhoods are less funded than their counterparts in white neighborhoods. To fix things—especially something as complex and interconnected as racism—we have to understand how they came to be and how they operate now.

"Well, this is all more complex than I thought." I was sitting with the executive director of a large nonprofit who had just gone through the definitions above in a leadership session. "I have to be honest: I knew about interpersonal racism and a little about structural racism, though I never could have defined it for someone else, but institutional racism was entirely new to me." I let her pause and absorb the feelings that were clearly washing over her: a little overwhelm, but also a sense of energy. Her eyes darted between her computer and the window. I could tell she was still examining the picture we had constructed as we connected the dots between the types of racism and the issues we face as individuals and organizations. A minute or so went by before I spoke: "May I ask what you're thinking about as this soaks in?"

She opened her mouth, then closed it. She opened her mouth again. "I guess I'm a bit shocked, and maybe a little frustrated, by how many dimensions there are to racism. When I thought about the work we needed to do here, at our organization, I really believed there was a clear path for us to do better. I knew it would take work. Now I see so many more layers, but I totally get it." In that moment I knew that she recognized that her newfound understanding would benefit her organization in so many more ways than she had expected. It gave her clarity and a deeper sense of what was operating not only at her institution, but also in her community and with her staff.

We Are Far Behind

While it was published decades ago, a speech given by Dr. Martin Luther King Jr. at Stanford University in 1967, titled "The Other America," is so, so relevant today.[16] It captures the urgency I feel

---

[16] Dr. Martin Luther King, "The Other America," accessed July 29th, 2022, https://www.crmvet.org/docs/otheram.htm.

about everything that's going on right now. He said, "There are those, and they are often sincere people, who say to Negroes and their allies in the white community, that we should slow up and just be nice and patient and continue to pray, and in a hundred or two hundred years the problem will work itself out because only time can solve the problem. I think there is an answer to that myth. And it is that time is neutral. It can be used either constructively or destructively. And I'm absolutely convinced that the forces of ill-will in our nation, the extreme rightists in our nation, have often used time much more effectively than the forces of good will."

The argument that progress will come with time is simply incorrect. If time alone is enough, we'd see more progress. Yet, here we are in the following circumstances:

- In the history of this country, we've had only eleven Black US Senators. You read that correctly: In 232 years, we have had eleven Black senators.

- In 2021, 34 percent of Black people reported feeling unfairly treated in the workplace due to race or ethnicity in the past year, and 42 percent felt unfairly treated in the past five years. Of those reporting being treated unfairly, 72 percent said it happened between one and five times, so these are almost never isolated incidents.[17]

- In a 2020 Gallup poll, 32 percent of Black adults said that in the past year people had acted as if they were "better than you," while 25 percent said people had acted as if "you were not smart." And 9 percent of Black adults reported having explicitly been called a name or insulted.[18]

- The Federal Reserve reported that in the first quarter of 2022,

---

[17] https://shrm.org/ResourcesAndTools/tools-and-samples/toolkits/Documents/TFAW21_CostOfInjustice.pdf.

[18] Camille Lloyd, "Black Adults Disproportionately Experience Microaggressions," *Gallup*, July 15, 2020, https://news.gallup.com/poll/315695/black-adults-disproportionately-experience-microaggressions.aspx.

> the average family wealth for white families is four times that of Black families and 4.3 times that of Hispanic families.[19]
>
> - At the end of 2022, home ownership rates in the United States, a significant contributor to wealth, were only 44 percent for Black people compared to 74 percent for non-Hispanic whites.[20]
>
> The reality is that if we don't see change, antiracism, and racial inequity as a collective responsibility, we'll never get to the place where we can solve any of it. Time doesn't make change; we do.

Part of the genius of systemic racism is that it is everywhere and yet most people don't know how badly it affects people, interactions, and outcomes. Racism makes me think very carefully about everyday things, like driving in my car, where I choose to eat dinner, and where I go for vacation. I don't feel comfortable getting in my car in St. Paul, Minnesota, and driving to a quaint small town to visit a friend's cabin. That doesn't mean that I won't do it, but I always think about a potential negative outcome. Take swimming, for another example: For decades law enforcement used fire hoses to control Black crowds, and Blacks were flat-out denied access to public swimming pools by whites even after integration laws were enacted. So, you know what? Water isn't always relaxing for us. Dogs are another possible trigger for Black people because slave catchers and law enforcement used them as weapons during the civil rights era. Our history is in our bones and our memories, and it changes the way we move around and feel within spaces. Security dogs at airports make me feel extra uncomfortable—something that likely

---

[19] Ana Hernández Kent and Lowell R. Ricketts, "Racial and Ethnic Household Wealth Trends and Wealth Inequality," July 11, 2022, *Federal Reserve Bank of St. Louis*, https://www.stlouisfed.org/institute-for-economic-equity/the-real-state-of-family-wealth/racial-and-ethnic-household-wealth.

[20] "Housing and Homeownership: Homeownership Rates," *St. Louis Fed*, https://fred.stlouisfed.org/release/tables?eid=784188&rid=296, accessed November 15, 2022.

never occurred to the person at the airport who made the decision to use dogs without considering how that might affect a group of people. I'm not saying that every Black person hates water and dogs, but I am saying that a group's history with particular aspects of our society, no matter how innocent those aspects may seem, can drastically change how the group's members engage in ways that might make little sense to others. Individuals of other races have their own traumas and triggers too. You won't understand them unless you make the effort.

If you don't deepen your understanding of race and racism, you may perpetuate the harm that's been caused up until now—maybe unwillingly, but acting from ignorance is no less damaging. In fact, it can be worse. BIPOC can tell when someone isn't even trying to understand. We can feel how many people are willfully ignorant and then turn around and say, "But I didn't know!" Here's the thing: you could have known. You *can* know. Racism happens around you *every day*. Even if you can't see it, it is there. Denying, ignoring, or disbelieving it doesn't make it untrue. If you're reading this book, you know it's out there: if you want to be an accomplice, you'll work continually to address your ignorance.

Remember that the arbiter of what is racist is always the person experiencing the racist act and never the person committing the act. Intent goes right out the door the minute someone says that the *impact* was racist. I know some people feel a certain way about this—attacked, offended, misunderstood, angry. They say, "What about…?" or, "That's not fair…" What if we spent all that energy instead on trying to understand the impact and learning how to do better? It's not so hard to convert your defensiveness to deepening. You can say, "Can you tell me more? I want to be able to understand the situation as you do." Instead of saying "I don't see it that way" when your action is perceived as racist, you can say, "I didn't perceive my actions that way. How you're experiencing this is very different from what I intended, and I don't want that to happen again. Can you help me understand it from your perspective?" When you ask questions, you're immediately in a different headspace than when you lock into your existing perspective.

Racism, in all of its forms, affects people's health. In 2020, the American Medical Association (AMA) declared racism a public health threat: "The AMA recognizes that racism negatively impacts and exacerbates health inequities among historically marginalized communities. Without systemic and structural-level change, health inequities will continue to exist, and the overall health of the nation will suffer."[21] This means that every BIPOC person experiences greater or compounding health issues simply because of their race. Piled on top of that, microaggressions or racism at work can make individuals feel unsafe and guarded, which reduces their ability to do their best work. When people are in survival mode, they can't participate with their whole self or at their fullest capacity without exerting extra effort. Look around and recognize that this is happening to the people at your workplace. They are probably struggling, just as I struggled to feel comfortable at my past jobs, and that struggle is likely invisible; it is having to let racialized comments roll off their backs and wondering whether their ability will be questioned due to race. They are having problems *that you can fix*. In fact, it's your responsibility to fix them by declaring your commitment to understanding how race is impacting people, allowing people to name their struggles directly and honestly, and then creating better and clearer pathways for BIPOC at your company.

Racism negatively impacts white folks too. Your biases and assumptions stand between you and people of color, and your beliefs will continue to separate you from others so long as you're moving through the world unaware of how others experience your relationships or interactions. This unawareness is palpable in how white people responded to the murder of George Floyd. Many were

---

[21] Kevin B. O'Reilly, "AMA: Racism Is a Threat to Public Health," *American Medical Association,* November 16, 2020, https://www.ama-assn.org/delivering-care/health-equity/ama-racism-threat-public-health.

surprised or shocked that it happened; Black people were not. Many didn't know what to say about it (as evidenced by Representative Nancy Pelosi's absurd and grossly uninformed comment thanking Mr. Floyd for giving his life to the cause). And many had no idea what to do to change the circumstances that allowed the murder to happen in the first place. Leaders wanted to make statements but didn't know what to say. Companies wanted to take a stand, but often their words and actions showed Black people that they don't understand the complexity of the problems. White folks haven't exhibited a full understanding of our collective circumstance, and, subsequently, they don't have the knowledge, understanding, or social capital to make change. This deficiency lies at the root of our issues: Most white people think they know what's up when it comes to race, but they don't. And they don't even know they're deficient, so they get double the impact.

Racism harms white people in more specific ways as well. All-white or mostly white teams don't know or understand their diverse customer base, which limits innovation and market potential for the products and services they're developing. Companies lose access to the skills and experience of diverse talent because their biases or white standards prevent them from seeing potential in and hiring certain job candidates. Racism harms business owners and state and federal legislators who fight against a living minimum wage because they're missing out on the potential spending power of the BIPOC citizens who would significantly benefit from it.

It's also something more subtle. When I reflect with leadership teams about the ways racism impacts their business, they often can't point to a specific and obvious harm. And I understand that; racism is complex and works behind the scenes, so it's difficult to pull the curtain and say, Here are four ways our business is suffering. But I still push the conversation because having a sense of how you, your team, and your company are affected is an important opt-in moment.

One of my clients said, "Looking back, I know there are

opportunities I missed because I didn't know what I didn't know." Recently, an HR director told me that she had believed the lack of BIPOC was a pipeline problem but now believed otherwise—it was a racism issue, not a pipeline issue.

Another client shared a very humbling reflection that had been haunting him for a while: "A few years back, I was hiring for a director-level job in my division. After several rounds of interviews, the final candidates were a Black woman and a white woman. I ended up offering the job to the white woman. I didn't think about race at the moment, as far as I could tell. But after the new director was in the position for about four months, I realized she was a terrible fit. We were constantly miscommunicating, and I was struggling with how we were going to make it work. She could tell; I could tell. And it was then, as I was so frustrated about the dynamic, that I started to think carefully about why I hadn't offered the job to the other candidate, the Black woman. Looking back, with some distance and with this person in the role who was obviously not going to work out, I could see that the other candidate was a much stronger fit for the role, but I think I was intimidated by her. I wondered what might happen if she ever disagreed with me or got upset with me in the workplace." He glanced at me, and then looked away. "I believe I let my unfamiliarity with and beliefs about Black people get in the way. I hired the white woman because I thought we'd 'get each other.'" I nodded at him; he was being really open and vulnerable and frankly saying what most of my white clients won't admit, at least out loud.

He went on, "I wish I would have given the other woman a chance. I am embarrassed I did that." But then his eyes brightened a little. "I can't fix that, I know, but once I realized that I was letting my biases get in the way, I worked really hard against them. I started hiring people who weren't like me at all, hoping that different perspectives would make the team stronger. And now we have a pretty diverse team." He was right: I didn't expect a story like this from this particular client because, more than most, he seemed to have a handle on the hiring side of racial equity. He concluded, "It wasn't a high point for me to realize that, but it was definitely a turning point. I still think about that other candidate, and it reminds me of all the ways we might be letting things happen without knowing it."

ANTI-BLACKNESS IS ITS OWN FORM OF DISCRIMINATION

Now I'm going to turn it up a notch and complicate what you might just be starting to understand about race and racism. There is nuance in what it means to be nonwhite in the United States and the varying ways different groups are perceived and receive support. For example, the COVID-19 Hate Crimes Act was passed in less than a year[22] in response to the horrid increase in anti-Asian crime during the pandemic. That is important legislation, *and yet*, Black people had to wait for more than a century (122 years, to be exact) to get anti-lynching legislation passed, with the Emmett Till Antilynching Act finally passing in 2022.[23] Of course I support both acts, *and* I also want to name the incredible anti-Black sentiment that we alone experience. The difference in how these two acts were passed is in part due to anti-Blackness.

Anti-Blackness is not distinct from racism, it's central to it: Racism is predicated on anti-Blackness because it's based on proximity to whiteness. Anti-Blackness is the name for the specific kind of racial prejudice directed toward Black people and all things Black. So, Black people (and people with darker skin) experience racism *and* anti-Blackness, which isn't necessarily the case for all historically underrepresented identities. While anti-Blackness is directed toward Black people specifically, it also affects people with a darker skin

---

[22] The bill was introduced on March 3, 2021 and passed on May 20, 2021. https://www.congress.gov/bill/117th-congress/senate-bill/937/actions

[23] "Anti-Lynching Petition," *History, Art, & Archives of the United State House of Representatives*, accessed July 29, 2022, https://history.house.gov/HouseRecord/Detail/15032448844?current_search_qs=%3FPreviousSearch%3D%26CurrentPage%3D1%26SortOrder%3DTitle.

experience or skin color that is more proximate to Black across many ethnic or cultural identities. For example, a study published in 2021 by Pew Research found, "A majority (62 percent) of Hispanic adults say having a darker skin color hurts Hispanics' ability to get ahead in the United States today at least a little. A similar share (59 percent) say having a lighter skin color helps Hispanics get ahead. And 57 percent say skin color shapes their daily life experiences a lot or some, with about half saying discrimination based on race or skin color is a 'very big problem' in the US today." The study also found that overall, darker-skinned Latinos experienced more discrimination than lighter-skinned Latinos.[24]

None of this is to say that lighter-skinned people have it easy, but it illustrates that anti-Blackness, "a two-part formation that both voids Blackness of value while systematically marginalizing Black people and their issues,"[25] is a specific subset of racism that piles more onto Black people and people with darker skin experiences. Anti-Blackness is the sentiment that pits everyone against Black people; it's the awful call that comes from inside the BIPOC house. As an accomplice, you have to recognize that while racism exists, so does anti-Blackness, and sometimes anti-Blackness is stronger than racism will ever be.

Anti-Blackness can be exhibited by anyone, and because of that, Black people (and people who are racialized as such) have a harder time in places and spaces where they are underrepresented. When they go into work, Black people have to deal with racism, anti-Blackness, the Black tax (see chapter 6), and race-related emotional labor. We manage our Black-specific experience in addition to our day-to-day responsibilities. That doesn't even take into account all the times we are confronted with Black death at the hands of law

---

[24] Luis Noe-Bustamante, Ana Gonzalez-Barrera, Khadijah Edwards, Lauren Mora and Mark Hugo Lopez, "Majority of Latinos Say Skin Color Impacts Opportunity in America and Shapes Daily Life," *Pew Research Center*, November 4, 2021, https://www.pewresearch.org/hispanic/2021/11/04/majority-of-latinos-say-skin-color-impacts-opportunity-in-america-and-shapes-daily-life/.

[25] https://www.racialequitytools.org/glossary

enforcement or violence against Black bodies—and we carry that with us. When we see people who could be our fathers, brothers, uncles, aunts, nieces, nephews, or niblings[26] killed, we feel it right in our hearts. So each day, these experiences are all part of the air we breathe and the life we live. In fact, a 2023 Indeed study found that 49% of Black workers were considering leaving their jobs.

Why am I bringing this up? Because Black employees in a predominantly white environment have to mentally prepare for all of the racialized incidents that happen to them at work, while white coworkers just pop on a blazer and brew some coffee. Black people suit up in armor to be ready for whatever the day might bring: deflecting microaggressions, politely reminding colleagues that it's not their job to fetch lunch, being ready to share their opinion when asked "How would Black people feel about this headline?" or explaining how braids work to the nth person. None of that could happen, or all of it could happen. Either way, we have to be ready for it. Anti-Blackness means that our existence is just harder. All of the time. Period.

"So, what do I do now?" Kathy asked. Again, she and I were discussing the survey answers that had rocked her. After a very human reaction of feeling disheartened and then taken aback at what her work was going to truly entail, she had recommitted. "We're going to use that feedback to deepen your understanding of race and racism *in your workplace*," I said. "We're going to use the commentary to start conversations with the people inside your organization who are experiencing racism." And we did. It wasn't a quick fix (there never is one, so I'm not going to share tips and tricks here!). We set a goal based on the feedback: to create an environment in which staff could trust each other and have open and honest conversations about their experiences. Over eight months we worked toward that goal with Kathy and the full staff, and month by month she earned some trust and developed a broader awareness of what was happening. I

---

[26] *Nibling* is a gender-neutral term used to refer to a child of one's sibling.

can't imagine that the conversations were easy for either party—the employees or Kathy—but I know they moved the needle.

Whether the definitions of race and the types of racism were new to you or a reminder, I hope you're now open to the ways race in this country has worked and continues to work, sometimes in invisible ways. When faced with the reality, complexity, and scale of race and racism, it may be easy to feel overwhelmed. At times, upon learning the history of the concept of race and the types of racism, folks become angry or sad. I want to reinforce that now is not the time to be overwhelmed. It's the time to feel alert and aware and to recognize that knowing this information—exactly what issues we face and the magnitude of their impact—means you can now be more useful as an accomplice. If you're like Kathy, you can take your shortcoming and use it to actively pursue a deeper analysis that leads you to question how race might be shaping the situations in which you find yourself.

PAUSE FOR AWARENESS AND ANALYSIS

- What do you know now that you didn't know before?
- Do conversations about race, in general, make you uncomfortable?
- As a leader, do you have cogent conversations with your teams about race?

- Do you think your team knows the differences between types of racism? If not, what could be gained by sharing this information with them?

- Where do you observe anti-blackness in your individual and organizational practices?

- In what ways do you see these types of racism play out daily at work or in your personal life?

- What are some of the negative impacts of racism on you, the people around you, and your organization?

- What does the data say about the presence of structural racism in your industry?

MOVE TO ACTION

Actively Integrate New Information as You Learn It

We often consume new information just to have new information. That might be fine when it comes to trivial topics like recipes or Rock 'n' Roll Hall of Fame inductees, but when it comes to the history and the topic of race, we have to recalibrate when we learn new information. When you learn new information while engaging with people, questions you should be asking yourself are:

- What did I just learn? *This is a way to synthesize and summarize it for yourself.*

- How does what I learned impact me as a person? *This helps you investigate the information in relation to yourself—and to strengthen your self-awareness.*

- How does what I learned impact others around me? *This helps you build your empathy meter and consider the differences between yourself and others.*

- What kind of support might people need based on what I just learned, and what can I do to support those people?

When we learn new things, the final step is reprogramming or reconditioning ourselves to move to action around what we're learning, rather than simply absorbing the information and, after accumulating perspectives or facts, saying, "I don't know what to do with any of that!" As things come in, and as things become more apparent, how can you use what you're learning to inform how you move through the world?

CHAPTER 3: WHITE SUPREMACY CULTURE IS ALWAYS AT PLAY

The Way Things Are is Not the Way Things Have to Be

What enables race, racism, and racialization to persist despite the harm they do to everyone? White supremacy culture. White supremacy culture is the invisible behaviors, beliefs, and order of things around us that inform large and small things. It is so woven into our daily lives that it might not feel like a culture at all; it might feel like "the way things are." But it is indeed a culture, and it informs all parts of life in this country, often without us being entirely aware of it. It's important to see it for what it is because the longer these cultural norms exist, the harder they will be to see. As of now, we're going on a few hundred years of this norm, so seeing it isn't easy. But we're going to start in this chapter.

The words *white supremacy* may evoke images of the Ku Klux Klan, swastikas, or any number of hate groups. But, like racism, white supremacy culture takes more forms than just these overt and explicit ones.

WHITE SUPREMACY CULTURE—DISTINCT FROM WHITE SUPREMACY OR WHITE SUPREMACISTS—IS THE SUBTLER EXPRESSION

OF A BELIEF THAT THE WHITE WAY IS THE RIGHT WAY.

In this chapter, I talk about the culture, which looks very different from the clans and robesmen. While we are not all white supremacists, we all—white people, Asian people, Black and brown people—participate in and perpetuate white supremacy culture because it is the invisible waters in which we swim. White supremacy culture is a political, economic, and cultural system in which:

- white people overwhelmingly control power and material resources;
- conscious and unconscious ideas of white superiority and entitlement are widespread;"
- relations of white dominance and non-white subordination are daily reenacted across a broad array of institutions and social settings.[27]

It is the systems and structures built to preserve, maintain, and advance whiteness. Now, whiteness here isn't white skin; it's white ways of being. Whiteness shows up in what is deemed respectable, normal, acceptable, appropriate, or comfortable. When we think about white supremacy culture, let's just call it the state of things.

THE BAROMETER OF COMFORT IS SET TO WHITE IN THIS COUNTRY.

Period. My colleague Carmen Morgan has been known to say this. Systems, processes, behavioral expectations, and ways of being are all set to favor white people because they were designed by and for

---

[27] Frances Lee Ansley, *Stirring the Ashes: Race Class and the Future of Civil Rights Scholarship*, 74 Cornell L. Rev. 993 (1989).

them. Whatever white people in power have put in place has had white interests and perspectives at its heart. The overarching belief is thus that BIPOC have to emulate whiteness in order to fit in, or actively reject it and suffer the consequences of being outsiders. And those consequences can be uncomfortable, discouraging, dangerous, or even deadly.

The thing about white supremacy culture is that it doesn't allow anyone else to fit in. Again, the number-one thing I hear from BIPOC is that they feel like they can't show up as their full selves at work. That may mean styling their hair in a particular way, not bringing foods from their culture for lunch because they would stand out, or avoiding words and phrases that might seem "too Black." The culture—at work and beyond—hasn't been amended, or it is not inclusive enough, for them to feel like they can show up as their full selves. Every workday, they are trying to lean into a culture that doesn't fit them. It's like trying to put on a pair of pants that are too small. You can't button them; you can't bend over; you can't do . . . anything. BIPOC, even when we're trying our best just to be ourselves, always have to consider whiteness because it's everywhere and in everything. So, it's like double work—we're trying to understand it and work within it even though we know it's nearly impossible to do so. And if you choose to work in a place where you're the only BIPOC, God help you; you're doing triple time because you're the token: and you're likely being asked (and sometimes answering) all the questions about race-related topics. It's hard to exist in spaces when that is how you have to behave, interact, and show up.

White supremacy culture is rampant in workplace settings. We can see this in *Women in the Workplace 2022*, a survey by Lean In and McKinsey & Company, of more than 40,000 employees from 333 organizations that employ more than 12 million people total. The study found that:

- 55 percent of Black women leaders report having their judgment questioned by others in the past year compared to 39 percent of all women leaders.

- 38 percent of Black women have been mistaken for someone at a lower level whereas only 26 percent of all women leaders have had that experience.

The State of Black Women in Corporate America, a 2020 Lean In and McKinsey & Company study that drew on years of data from their annual Women in the Workplace surveys, found:

- 49 percent of Black women feel that their race or ethnicity will make it harder for them to get a raise, promotion, or chance to get ahead, compared to just 3 percent of white women and 11 percent of women overall.

- Black women are much less likely than their non-Black colleagues to interact with senior leaders at work. This lack of access is mirrored in a lack of sponsorship: less than a quarter of Black women feel they have the sponsorship they need to advance their career.

- More than 1 in 4 Black women have heard someone in their workplace express surprise at their language skills or other abilities; just 1 in 10 white women have had this experience.

- When surveying "onlys"—people who are the only person in a space of a particular gender and racial identity—49 percent of Black women feel under pressure to perform, compared to 21 percent of white men; 40 percent of Black women feel on guard, compared to 18 percent of white men; and 41 percent of Black women feel closely watched, compared to 15 percent of white men.[28]

---

[28] *The State of Black Women in Corporate America 2020,* Lean In, accessed November 17, 2022, https://leanin.org/research/state-of-black-women-in-corporate-america.

These studies show how Black women—a group exponentially impacted by white supremacy culture because of their gender and race—have it harder than other identity categories in just about every single way. The findings point to how hard Black women have to work just to be taken seriously, let alone advance—and this is the concept of Black tax in action. Black tax is the notion that Black people have to work two or three times as hard as their colleagues just to exist and advance in the workplace. You can't just be good at your job; you have to be great. You can't make mistakes, you must do things well and right the first time around, and you get no leeway if things go wrong. This tax prevents Black people from moving into leadership positions—they have to do so much more even to be considered for a role, let alone make it into the interview process.

White supremacy culture permeates our understanding of "professionalism" in particular. Almost everything that is considered "professional" is arbitrary and very much connected to a standard of white maleness inherent in white supremacy culture. This includes how individuals are expected to dress and do their hair and makeup; how people are supposed to interact with others; what can be said and what cannot be said; who gets recognized for what; who gets access to what information, meetings, and people; and top-down leadership standards and respected leadership behaviors. We have all experienced these standards, and maybe some of us comfortably fit within some of the expectations. But the reality is that the expectations are set to reward conforming white males, and others who benefit from professionalism do so by mimicking these behaviors or standards.

These standards are so powerful that, as a young girl, I was specifically taught the strategy of speaking in such a way that my race couldn't be detected by what I said or how I said it. I call this "putting on my best white-lady voice." And it was especially important for succeeding at work. In fact, it was an important inflection point for me because I realized that speaking in a very particular way—a white-acceptable way—was essential to my success. In my childhood I thought, "If I don't do this, I will starve." This idea that how we speak directly correlates with our aptitude or capabilities plays out in all kinds of ways in our culture. African American Vernacular English (AAVE or AAE)—formerly known as Black English Vernacular or Vernacular Black English among sociolinguists and previously commonly called Ebonics outside the academic community—is not considered an acceptable way of speaking. Volume, word choices, tone, and storytelling style are policed as well, especially in a professional setting. According to the linguist Sharese King and psychologist Katherine D. Kinzler, "Like any dialect, AAE is a part of the cultural fabric of its speakers and has its own accent and rule-governed grammar. But despite its legacy in shaping American culture, this historic language is often derided as ungrammatical and linguistically less than other forms of American speech. The result is that AAE speakers are denigrated and discredited based on their speech."[29]

Black hair is another example. US states have had to pass legislation so that Black people don't get discriminated against because of the texture of their natural hair. This is because Black hair, as it grows out of people's head, isn't considered professional according to norms established by and for white people. Black people are expected to straighten it, lighten it, or otherwise change it so white folks feel more comfortable with how it looks (i.e., more like white hair). I know Black women who email their teams before showing up to work with a new hairstyle to keep people from asking questions about how they do their hair, which just distracts from their actual work responsibilities. It took me years to simply wear my braids and not care what people thought.

Having to consciously change who we are, or decide not to, adds pressures and stress to your life, all to try to fit into a space

---

[29] Sharese King and Katherine D. Kinzler, "Op-Ed: Bias against African American English speakers is a pillar of systemic racism," *Los Angeles Times*, July 14, 2020, https://www.latimes.com/opinion/story/2020-07-14/african-american-english-racism-discrimination-speech.

that you inherently cannot fit into. A dear friend of mine who is also Black once said, "You are oftentimes, without your permission and unwillingly, pulled into a situation where you're literally—I say it like this intentionally—on the block again, being sold, evaluated, criticized, and critiqued. And oftentimes at work, that means it's in the context of what's supposed to be a safe space or an exchange of thoughts or a fun exercise." And I couldn't agree more. The reality is, all the things that feel normal are not. They are a specific culture, designed and created in a particular way.

NOTHING'S "NORMAL"—THERE'S NO SUCH THING. AND IN AN INCLUSIVE WORLD, YOU DISAVOW TERMS LIKE *NORMAL* BECAUSE IT DOESN'T EXIST.

That's right, a single homogeneous way of being does not exist.

The confluence of all of these small, seemingly trivial things adds up to a lived reality in which some people are constantly contorting or policing themselves (it's ingrained at this point) just to be considered acceptable or avoid being fired. While attitudes may be shifting and we may be making some headway in changing professional standards, especially after COVID and a year of many people working from home, I think we all know there is far more progress to make.

EXAMINING WHITE SUPREMACY CULTURE

Let's look more closely at white supremacy culture. In their seminal article "White Supremacy Culture," originally from *Dismantling Racism: A Workbook for Social Change Groups*, authors Kenneth Jones and Tema Okun of dRworks list fifteen characteristics of white supremacy culture. I encourage you to seek out their work in full at http://www.whitesupremacyculture.info, where they have longer descriptions and in-depth explanations. Please read their materials and donate to support their ongoing work, which has helped bring to light what is often invisible, especially at work or in professional environments.

Nine of Jones and Okun's characteristics of white supremacy culture are:

Fear — White supremacy culture's number-one strategy is to make us afraid. When we are afraid, we lose touch with our power and become more easily manipulated by the promise of an illusory safety.

One right way — The belief there is one right way to do things. This is connected to the belief in an objective "perfect" that is both attainable and desirable for everyone and to the belief that I am qualified to know what the perfect right way is for myself and others.

Either/or and binary thinking — Reduces the complexity of life and the nuance of our relationships with each other and all living things into either/or, yes or no, right or wrong in ways that reinforce urgency, one-right-way perfectionist thinking, and abuse of power.

Denial and defensiveness — The habit of denying and defending against the ways in which white supremacy and racism are produced and our individual or collective participation in that production.

Right to comfort and fear of conflict — The internalization that I or we have a right to comfort, which means we cannot tolerate conflict, particularly open conflict.

Worship of the written word — Honoring only what is written, and even then only what is written to a narrow standard, even when what is written is full of misinformation and lies. An erasure of the wide range of ways we communicate with each other and all living things.

Urgency — Applying the urgency of racial and social justice to our everyday lives in ways that perpetuate power imbalance and disregard for our need to breathe and pause and reflect.

Individualism — Our cultural story that we make it on our own, without help, while pulling ourselves up by our own bootstraps, is a toxic denial of our essential interdependence and the reality that we are all in this, literally, together.

Progress is bigger, more — The assumption that the goal is always more and bigger with an emphasis on what we can "objectively" measure as more valuable than the quality of our relationships to all living beings.

Some white people have a difficult time understanding white supremacy culture because they take it as a personal attack. I assure you, it is not that. When I share Jones and Okun's article with my clients, I inevitably hear, "But some of this is just how things are!" To which I say: exactly. It is entrenched to the degree that we don't see it as intentionally designed or as something we can change. I know it can be challenging to see a list of things that feel "natural" but perpetuate something terrible, like oppression. The bottom line is that white supremacy culture means one person's "normal" can be completely at odds with someone else's everyday lived experience.

I ask that, first, you believe that what is listed above is accurate and harmful to some people. No one has time for lies or wants to make others feel like crap; we just want the systems holding some people back to be seen for what they are. Second, I ask that you reflect on them without centering yourself. Remember, this isn't me (or anyone) saying that you, personally, are a white supremacist if you have some of these tendencies as an individual or if they're present in your work culture. It's not about *you*—white supremacy culture is everywhere.

If you're struggling to understand the connection between these characteristics and whiteness or how these tenets could be difficult to conform to, you need to talk to others, unpack what's written here, do some research, and spend time examining alternate ways of doing things. A clear understanding of white supremacy culture is central to your accompliceship journey.

Let's talk about some of the ways the above characteristics play out inside an organization. Earlier I shared the example of Black hair, which relates to comfort and people wanting things to be familiar instead of celebrating and making space for differences. Another example is teams of people giving others Western-sounding nicknames because they can't pronounce their colleague's given name, like saying "Sam" instead of "Samoka." Trust me, if you can say *Tchaikovsky*, you can say *Samoka*. Either/or thinking shows up when only some holidays are represented on the company calendar. There is no reason to choose a particular religion to represent via default days off, and yet many companies show a clear preference. And space is simply not made for behaviors or needs that are perceived to be outside the norm. Prayer rooms are not as common as breastfeeding rooms. Providing access for people with invisible disabilities is rarely planned. Do you have a culture in which people can tell you that they're not neurotypical and not feel backlash? Stigmas around therapy, counseling, and coaching—all things associated with not meeting expectations—could become part of a culture that appreciates and encourages growth and self-awareness. I often tell my clients that one quick test of your culture is to look at whether BIPOC employees share job openings with their networks. If they do, that tells you that they are comfortable enough to invite someone else into that workspace. If they don't, well, that too tells you something (though not everything) about how they feel.

The truth is, you can't create an inclusive culture at your workplace without wading into the controversial waters of white supremacy culture. This examination helps in two ways. De-centering white supremacy culture—and yourself, if you are white—is the first piece. The only way to dislodge the tenacity of this culture is to learn about the nuances of your part in a systemic problem and understand how that problem manifests in daily life. Second, white supremacy culture is the most significant barrier to inclusion; it is the opposite of inclusion. It will get in the way over and over again unless you face it head-on. Here are some ways it might be creeping into your workplace:

- Your company culture hasn't evolved beyond the perspectives of or with inputs aside from the (usually white) founders. This is classic one-right-way thinking. The personalities or culture of the small group of founders dictates everything, leaving no room for others.

- You hire people who fit your culture rather than contribute to your culture. A culture "fit" means everyone is comfortable and familiar; the more people are alike, the less likely you have to think about hegemony.

- Leadership says, "I'm just impatient." Urgency often masquerades as impatience or the need to move fast in business. I hear this from clients. *All. The. Time.* Leaders will often write off this behavior as just "how they are." If you see yourself in this comment, I suggest you consider that however you "are," you can also be a different way if you want.

- Decisions that affect everyone are made by a select few people with no input from others. It's then assumed that because the select few leaders made the decision, it must be the right decision. Any pushback or feedback is discouraged or rejected. This is related to one-right-way thinking, but with a paternalistic twist. When anyone thinks they can make decisions for everyone without asking for others' opinions, it smacks of "I know best."

- The leadership team takes DEIAA training but doesn't tell, or provide it for, staff. This lack of transparency is embedded in fear—fear of messing up, of doing the wrong thing, or of not knowing how to do something well.

- Your leadership or client-facing team is all white, while the people behind the scenes are more diverse. Lack of representation often comes down to white being the barometer of comfort, so highly visible roles are filled by people who can maintain this comfort.

- You don't have partner programs to help young employees chart the best course possible for them at your company. This is distinct from a new-hire buddy system in which the new employee is told how things work. This is individualism at work: a system built on the notion that hard work alone is what you need to advance in a complex, interdependent workplace.

- People don't take breaks, vacations, time off, or other space for themselves to do things other than work—and that's rewarded by accolades or promotions. This is quantity over quality coming through.

- Promotions or choice projects are given to people based on connections rather than merit. Again, people are most comfortable around people just like them, so they make business decisions based on who they want to chat with, not who is doing the best work.

- People say, "We need to write everything down—documentation is king." I ask, why is writing valued over other forms of communication?

- The refrain "We have to move fast; we can't take too much time to do this, or we'll lose our opportunity" is frequently used. What are you missing out on when you make everything urgent rather than take your time?

- A guiding mantra is "There's no room for mistakes." If you're always focusing on *bigger* and *more*, how do we learn from our past behaviors?

- And here is a real kicker: "We do it this way because it's how we've always done it, and it works." What if what you've always done—the "right way"—is limiting, exclusive, and only works for some people?

Does any of this sound like you or your business or organization? If you're attempting to create a culture of inclusion, one in which everyone can show up with their full selves, you will have to open your perspective to other ways of operating.

We have to have those uncomfortable conversations about white supremacy at work and in our actions, or white leaders and leadership will become obsolete. Beyond the moral imperative to do better, you simply won't be able to lead a team of diverse people if you don't start dealing with the unspoken and the uncomfortable things. The accomplice takes the risk of saying to themselves, "You know what? I actually need to do something different; I need to engage with this controversial stuff." Don't you want to go to a job where you don't feel like you have to walk on eggshells around issues of race, gender, and inclusion in general? Don't you want to know what to say to your team when murders (specifically gun violence) happen? Because Black and Brown people know how to have these conversations; we know the language of oppression better than white folks do, and we can simply start our own businesses and leave the languishing white companies to their static culture. If business leaders don't change their circumstances and culture, then they'll remain uncomfortable, underprepared, and isolated. I know that sounds threatening, but I don't mean it to be. It is simply the direction of things.

The truth of the matter is, white supremacy culture, like racism, hurts everyone. It limits the white experience by keeping people confined to particular ways of seeing the world and common ways of behaving. While the culture maintains whiteness as a source of power, the culture isn't easy for any one person to abide by. It doesn't behoove anyone to be such a rugged individual that they can't ask for help or work with others toward a larger purpose. Each of the qualities above may serve us sometimes; each is also very limiting at other times. This culture was designed for whiteness, and in particular white, cisgender men, which means it is limiting even to them. Each and every one of us must look at the way things are and imagine how they could be.

PAUSE FOR AWARENESS AND ANALYSIS

- What's resonating about what you read in this chapter?

- What do you know now that you didn't know before?

- Of the white supremacy culture characteristics above, which two do you most see in yourself and your actions? How will you start to dismantle them in your behavior?

- What white supremacy culture characteristics do you see in other people at your workplace?

- What white supremacy culture characteristics do you see at play in the systems, policies, or culture at your workplace?

- What are potential solutions for the ways white supremacy culture shows up in your life and organization?

How can you commit to making this an ongoing conversation for yourself? Because this definitely isn't a one-and-done.

MOVE TO ACTION

Hold Yourself Accountable for Naming It

In part, white supremacy culture is so pervasive because we don't talk about it. Its perpetuation relies on us never speaking of it because we're either too uncomfortable or too defensive to engage in that conversation. You have to name it, and you have to be very clear about the fact that it exists and what it looks like in your existing environment.

- Share the characteristics above in team or staff meetings.

- Openly discuss characteristics that show up in your workplace or in common behaviors. Even if your workplace does not exhibit all the characteristics, acknowledge the ones that do appear to raise awareness and adjust behaviors as needed.

- Prepare for pushback by finding counterexamples of cultures, workplaces, or behaviors that are effective outside the constraints of white supremacy culture.

- Encourage people to observe and name characteristics in real time to foster a culture of accountability around correcting these behaviors.

Naming things, in ongoing and open dialogues, will create a sense of clarity around the culture. This is crucial: If you don't make it obvious, it will be like trying to fight the Invisible Man. If you don't call it out, you won't face it, and you have to face it to conquer it as it unfolds. Some pieces of your culture may be fine now, but they won't be in six months. And that's okay—you will learn, grow, and make space for more people to bring more of themselves to your workplace. But you have to do all of those things and commit to ongoing observation of your culture; otherwise, the crappy parts will just keep returning.

If you're not sure how inclusive or exclusive your organization's culture is right now, ask people. It's important to explicitly ask because, I assure you, you don't know everything about your organization's culture right now, especially as it pertains to inclusion, belonging, and how people around you actually feel about any DEIAA efforts you're making. I have witnessed every one of my executive clients realize that they don't actually know every aspect of their company (whether they own it or just run it), and it's an important turning point in their commitment to this work. Remember James and Kathy? As attentive and astute leaders, they were certain they had a solid grasp on how their colleagues and staff felt about their workplace. But I have seen the sad and frustrated faces after leaders finally ask people what their experiences are and how they feel about work. Almost every leader in today's business environment has done a 360-degree-feedback exercise. Use that exercise on your culture, include everyone in the process, and be prepared for feedback. It will reveal what is working and what is not.

CHAPTER 4: POWER AND PRIVILEGE ARE YOUR PATHS TO ACTION

We All Need to Be in Service to Others

What was your biggest worry this week? Was any part of it rooted in your racial identity? Can you think of anything that your racial identity prevented or enabled? Aside from your biggest worries, can you:

> Use sidewalks with little to no difficulty?

> Move through most rooms or public spaces easily?

> Find a public restroom that aligns with your gender expression or identity?

> Go to a doctor's appointment without worrying about how the doctor will treat you?

> Use the water coming out of the faucets in your home without considering its quality?

> Engage in day-to-day activities knowing that there is no impending legislation that may take away one of your fundamental rights?

These questions point to ways that some of us may experience privilege without being entirely conscious of it.

DEVELOPING A PERSISTENT AND CONSISTENT AWARENESS OF YOUR PRIVILEGE IS FOUNDATIONAL FOR YOUR PRACTICE BECAUSE YOUR PRIVILEGE POINTS TO WHERE YOU CAN MAKE AN IMPACT. PRIVILEGE IS WHAT YOU POSSESS; POWER IS THE ACTION YOU TAKE.

Read that again: *Privilege is what you possess; power is the action you take.* Privilege is inherent in who you are, and it is unearned; power is how you use that privilege to move to action.

Like racism, privilege operates on interpersonal, institutional, and systemic levels. Social privilege grants a special right, advantage, or benefit to members of a dominant group at the expense of historically excluded groups. In a US context, Christians, cisgender heterosexuals, and white people are a few examples of socially privileged groups. Social privilege is unearned and given to individuals within dominant groups whether they want it or not, and it is kept from individuals in historically excluded groups, no matter how hard they may work to earn privilege. No one with white skin worked hard to achieve that skin color; it's a conferred status that they had no choice in. No one should feel guilty because of this, but no one should feel superior because of it either. As it plays out in everyday life, privilege only benefits the dominant group and, as such, perpetuates the status quo. Everything that deviates from the status quo of the dominant, privileged group is considered different or other. But let me be clear: we all have some privilege. Each of us has access to some aspects of our society that someone else does not have.

In a social and work context, privilege often isn't about receiving perks or benefits based explicitly on your identity or other factors. It's most often experienced as the absence of barriers and obstacles because of your identity or other factors. No one gives you a job or promotion *because* you're white, Christian, heteronormative, or a person without a visible disability. But companies interview individuals with Black-sounding names less frequently than individuals with white-sounding names.[30] Some companies refuse to provide access to prayer spaces or clothing for members of some religious or cultural groups. Some companies don't create inclusive bathrooms, forcing employees to choose between two options (men and women) when neither is fitting for them. Most companies have a singular onboarding experience regardless of learning style. You may never have noticed these things if you have certain kinds of privilege; you might be sheltered from these negative or exclusionary experiences.

Power is the ability to do something or act in a particular way.[31] When you have power, you are in a position to take action. In a work context, organizational hierarchy often grants power in the form of the ability to make change within the organization or to make a decision that could have an impact. While that sounds only like I'm talking about the bosses, we all have power to make decisions at work and in our personal lives. No matter what your role, you make decisions that can be acted on with an antiracist lens. If you buy lunch for a team, where are you purchasing the meal? How about patronizing a Black-owned restaurant? If you schedule appointments and meetings for people in higher positions than

---

[30] See "Are Emily And Greg More Employable than Lakisha And Jamal? A Field Experiment On Labor Market Discrimination," by Marianne Bertrand Sendhil Mullainathan, 2003 or "Whitened Résumés: Race and Self-Presentation in the Labor Market" by Sonia Kang, Katy DeCelles, András Tilcsik, and Sora Jun, 2016.

[31] The New Oxford American Dictionary (via Apple Dictionary)

you, how about granting access to people who may not otherwise get on the executives' calendars? If you write policies or processes, how about using inclusive language? These are all actions individuals make from positions of power. We may not have *all* of the power, but each of us has *some* power.

Truthfully, it was illuminating for me when I realized I had power and privilege. As a Black woman, I didn't consider how I could use it to help other people. But here are some ways that I experience privilege each day: I wake up in a home that I own, for which I was able to receive a loan because of my good credit history. I can step out of my bed with little difficulty because my legs and back allow me to do that; then I walk to the kitchen and fill a glass with drinkable water. I can see the morning light and hear the noise around me because my eyes and ears function as they were designed to. I can prepare breakfast and cut vegetables with relative ease because I have control over my motor skills. I can drive a car without adaptive equipment, and it gets me to stores that sell the types of whole foods I want to purchase, and I live in a metropolitan area with those amenities available. I have obtained a valid driver's license because I was given a birth certificate upon birth at a hospital. When out in public, I can use the public restrooms with no issue because my gender aligns with the sex I was assigned at birth. When people refer to me using pronouns, their assumptions match my own identity. I can read signage, manage loud or chaotic situations, and interact comfortably with strangers. When I go home in the evening, I don't worry about my electricity or gas being turned off because I am in an economically stable and predictable circumstance. Most of my monthly bills are on autopay. The air around my home is not contaminated to a greater degree than other parts of the city because I live in a residential area far from any manufacturing or industrialized businesses. If I make a last-minute decision to order food, I don't have to check my bank account to avoid disrupting the flow of my financial circumstances.

On the flip side, in 2021 I discussed with a mortgage loan officer whether I should refinance my home given the low interest rates. On the one hand, it was enticing to me; who doesn't like to save money, especially when it means paying less interest to a bank? But on the other hand, I was scared to even go down that road. I'm privileged to have all the things you're supposed to have to secure a good loan—a fantastic credit score, low revolving debt, a healthy savings account, and a thriving business—and I'm still scared about how I will be treated as a Black woman asking the historically racist banking industry for approval. The truth of it is, Black people don't experience the same privilege as others when it comes to financial and real-estate transactions. Here are all the concerns that went through my mind based on my lived experience as a Black woman:

- Will I actually get a low interest rate? History shows banks are more hesitant to extend favorable loan terms to Black people.

- Will my property be appraised accurately? An appraisal is often required for a refinance or purchase, and Black homes are routinely undervalued by appraisers simply because Black people own them.[32]

- Will adding my husband to the loan result in further discrimination because he is West African and his name reads as such?

- Will they require an invasive degree of proof of my ability to repay the loan because I own my business and am a Black woman?

---

[32] See Debra Kamin, "Widespread Racial Bias Found in Home Appraisals," *New York Times*, November 2, 2022, https://www.nytimes.com/2022/11/02/realestate/racial-bias-home-appraisals.html, Debra Kamin, "Black Homeowners Face Discrimination in Appraisals," *New York Times*, August, 25, 2020, https://www.nytimes.com/2020/08/25/realestate/blacks-minorities-appraisals-discrimination.html, and Andre M. Perry, Jonathan Rothwell, and David Harshbarger, "The devaluation of assets in Black neighborhoods," Brookings, November 27, 2018, https://www.brookings.edu/research/devaluation-of-assets-in-black-neighborhoods/.

The white loan officer was shocked at all the things I was rightly concerned about that she had never considered. And, frankly, I was shocked (and a bit angry) that she was so unaware. She was only surprised by my concerns because she had never encountered them; her racial identity shielded her from that reality, and she had not made herself aware of the systemic racism within the industry she had worked in for years. The wealth of information available about this very topic had never permeated her awareness, nor had she sought it out to better serve Black folks. It was very clear that she had no idea Black people were routinely and systematically lowballed in appraisals. I found it jarring that she could be completing real estate transactions without knowing the history of housing and housing discrimination in the city in which she was working. As leaders and managers, we cannot be this disconnected in areas of our supposed expertise. If you don't know what's really happening to other people in your industry and organization, are you actually an expert in your field?

But, like I said, privilege is often easier to see when you don't have it. I know that I can tell my white clients, and you (if you are white), that you have privilege, but my telling you doesn't make you see it. If you are BIPOC, I can illuminate all the ways we do have privilege despite being racialized every day. The bottom line is that we all have some power and we all have some privilege. I experience privilege every day; I also experience discrimination. The two are not mutually exclusive. Self-awareness of where we are immune and where we encounter obstacles will help us do the most good.

Privilege Doesn't Mean You Haven't Had Difficulty

I want to address a typical comeback that white people use in conversations about power and privilege. Folks will say, "But I had to work hard to get where I am. I wasn't handed my job, my house, or my education."

Yes, that is true. But when people talk about power and privilege, no one says you have exponential power, like the ThunderCats or She-Ra. We are saying that because you are white, your race has never impeded you from anything. Your life hasn't been harder specifically because of the color of your skin. No one is saying you've never had a hard time or faced challenging things. But the reality is that whatever has happened to you, your skin color wasn't an impediment to your subsequent success. And just as I can experience both privilege and discrimination, you can have an easier time because of your skin and a harder time in other areas of your life. It is not an either/or.

POWER AND PRIVILEGE ARE OUR PATHS TO IMPACT

Understanding our privilege is the only way to perceive the degree of inequity in our world and understand where and how we can use it to make a difference. Our privilege points to where we have more power than some others. When we understand it, we can begin to see and correct the systems that perpetuate inequity. Yet, privilege is hard for people to face. It cracks open a deep well of awareness that can be overwhelming. I think this is the most challenging part of the ally-to-accomplice journey. It can feel disheartening to realize all the ways you are comfortable because it means facing that some people are never comfortable in the same way. But that is precisely why we need strong white accomplices; if BIPOC or any historically excluded group could have solved these issues by ourselves, we would have. But here we are, and now we need white accomplices to start disrupting comfort.

When you understand your privilege, you will see obstacles that were invisible to you before, and you can use whatever power you have to take action. For example, if you have cisgender privilege, you can ask for inclusive bathrooms or pronoun training with little risk. As a heterosexual, cisgender woman, you can be a great accomplice to a transgender person in your workplace. As a white person, you can research inequitable hiring processes and then ask about the hiring process at your own workplace to find any unfair elements. Any white person on a team can amplify a BIPOC thought, observation, or idea; find out what their needs are; and be more sensitive. Important caveat, though: unless you have a relationship with a BIPOC colleague, do not walk up to someone and ask how you can amplify their needs. Just engage when you have the opportunity, such as recognizing when they are ignored or overlooked in a meeting. White folks have the power to do that every day, right now. And white folks can say things that other people can't get away with. They can speak up for BIPOC colleagues in ways that other people can't without retribution, like calling out racist comments, microaggressions, or harmful omissions such as not giving someone credit for their time and work.

One day, I received an email from a client named Sandra that read, "Do you know anyone who could help us with Asian cultural sensitivity training? We are producing [*insert name of big musical with anti-Asian stereotypes here*] in the spring, and I want to work with a consultant as we put it on."[33] I thought about it for a moment. She was a theater director who had been working with us for a while by that point. I was a little taken aback by the question. Why would they put on that show, of all shows? I was pretty peeved. However, in order to not put my foot in my mouth, I first consulted with some dear friends of mine who are Asian and work in the theater industry, and I asked whether, as a Black woman, I had the standing to tell my client that they can't really be embarking on an antiracist journey *and* produce [*anti-Asian musical*]—that is just too contradictory. I wondered if it was my place to take opportunities away from Asian-American theater artists who have, historically, had so few roles—especially as theaters were opening again after the pandemic shutdown. My friends gave me the go-ahead and thanked me for taking the risk of talking to my client about the issue.

---

[33] I'm not even going to name the show!

I sent an email back: "Hey, Sandra. Can we jump on a call and talk about this?" We scheduled something for later that week. When she picked up the phone, I took a deep breath and said, "Hey, as your coach and your friend, and as someone who's trying to help you through this work, can I be honest about something?" She said, "Sure, Seena." I continued, "You can't produce this musical. Listen, you're in the middle of doing antiracism work, and going forward with this musical will undo all of the work you've done. Also, I don't know if I can continue to work with you if you have the chance to do right and you don't. There will always be challenges that will require you to opt in and do the harder, but right, thing." I let out a long breath; these truth-telling conversations, no matter how sure I am of the message, are never easy, but I was deeply committed to using my relationship with her, and my social capital with the theater, to shed light on how hurtful running that show might be for some people.

I heard a heavy sigh on the other end of the line. "I knew it wasn't the right thing to do, but we already had it teed up before the pandemic and I was just going to go ahead and do it. We had already committed to the artists." Now, this didn't surprise me. It made me a little sad, but it didn't surprise me. Folks *know* when they're ignoring an antiracist opportunity; they just hope that this one time will be okay and believe that they'll do the right thing the next time. I said, "You know, you can put the artists in a different production."

We had a long conversation on how to change the programming, assessing the risk in every detail and planning the path forward. It was important to me that we follow each detail all the way through because any one of them could have easily become an excuse not to move to action. Even well-intentioned folks will use some of the most fixable reasons to not do the right thing.

"Now I just have to run all of this by Robert," Sandra anxiously said. Robert, the managing director, was her partner in making the decision and had also been in coaching with me. A few weeks went by, and in a session with both Sandra and Robert I asked, "So what did you all decide about [*anti-Asian musical*]?" Sandra began, "Well, I called Robert right after we spoke and…" Suddenly Robert cut her off. "Seena, I knew we shouldn't do that play, too, and I was also going to let it happen. I feel crappy that I would have let that show go on. But you're right: We can't. We canceled it."

I asked, "And how do you both feel about that change?"

"It was really hard at first," Sandra answered. "It required a lot of work for us to pivot, find a new production, recast and reschedule all of the various parts, and also keep communication open with the staff and actors so people understood why we did what we did. But I am so glad we did. That work was worth it, and I am relieved that we chose the path that was more aligned with our values."

In this situation, I used my power to tell a difficult truth to my client, and I used my privilege to call out that the play was anti-Asian. In turn, my client had power in her workplace: as the artistic director, she could change the programming. She had privilege that allowed her to raise concerns about the racist elements of the play and have the managing director's ear. Both directors had the privilege of leading an organization financially stable enough to pivot the lineup and still stay afloat. They had the power to rehire the actors slated for [*anti-Asian show*] and include them in other productions. We each *used* the power gained through privilege—we didn't just recognize we had it.

Now let me be clear: this is not a story about how awesome Seena is. Not at all. This is a story about how one person can make a difference and how it is our collective responsibility to help our friends and colleagues make the right decisions whenever the opportunity arises.

How are you going to use your power to take action? Have you been nervous about using your privilege, even when you know it's the right thing to do? Perhaps you've witnessed a microaggression or an inequitable decision in the moment and looked the other way, not because you don't care or don't understand, but because you were nervous. Maybe you're not sure you should be the one to stand up and point out the issue. I say, "You are always the one who should point out the issue. We all are." We should all expect the same from ourselves and fellow accomplices.

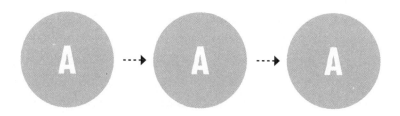

PAUSE FOR AWARENESS AND ANALYSIS

- What do you know now that you didn't know before?
- If you're a white person, do you think you'd have had the same successes if you were a Black person?
- Are you comfortable openly discussing your own power and privilege?
- In what ways do you experience privilege in your daily life?
- What are some ways that your colleagues may not experience the same privilege? Is there anything you can do to support them?
- How are you using your power and privilege for others?
- As a result of what you learned in this chapter, what are three concrete actions you want to take?

MOVE TO ACTION

Practice Moving from Guilt to Self-Awareness to Action

We are all conditioned by the information we were and are exposed to, the social and cultural environments we grew up in, and the history we experienced or learned along the way. Our parents and caretakers, friend groups, religion, culture, and geographic area all inform what we think and learn, and what we learn influences our behaviors and our identities. As you learn more about race and racism, you may find yourself asking, "How is it that as an adult, I don't know these things already?" or thinking, "I'm embarrassed that I thought our history was one thing, and now I'm learning it's more complicated." With these thoughts often come feelings of guilt or shame. We all want to be our best selves and to believe we are moving through the world with an awareness of others. Yet, exploring race can shine a light on our inadequacies. That's never comfortable.

Your practice of becoming an accomplice will continually introduce new ideas to the way you experience the world. And isn't that why we embark on personal learning journeys in the first place—to expand? Still, your lizard brain and muscle memory will have to contend with this new information. It's human nature for our conditioning to kick into defense when we learn something at odds with what we've always thought to be true. But that reaction can be just a *first* reaction—you don't have to stop at the defensiveness. I invite you to think about guilt and shame as opportunities not to shut down, but to move to action. Here's how you might do that:

- Spend ten seconds feeling guilty or ashamed or embarrassed or uncomfortable—feel it, you're human.

- Then spend a few minutes dwelling on awareness. Ask, "What is the new information I'm processing, and how can I add it to my world view and my catalog of what I know about the world?" Maybe you want to journal about it or have a conversation with someone who is on a similar journey.

- Finally, get moving: Ask, "What will I do better now that I know this new information?"

PART 2: CREATING YOUR BEST PRACTICE FOR ANTIRACIST LEADERSHIP

Part 1 deepened your understanding of the factors at play as you seek to address inequity and injustice. This is your foundation for the next part of being an accomplice: developing an ongoing antiracist practice that continuously increases your awareness, strengthens your analysis, and moves you to action. You can come back to this practice at every turn to answer "What would an accomplice do?" These guiding principles provide a framework for thinking, learning, and acting from a place that enables your best, most empathetic self to come forward and take risks on behalf of others.

Your Practice
Commit to a Race-First Lens

Defining practice question: How might race be playing into this situation?

Acknowledge Your Racial Identity

Defining practice question: How is *my* race impacting my interactions?

Define What You're Willing to Work For

Defining practice question: How can I continuously opt in to anti-racist action?

Get Curious

Defining practice question: What information or perspectives am I missing?

Engage with Difference

Defining practice question: How am I widening my aperture?

Take Risks

Defining practice question: Now that I know more, what can I do?

CHAPTER 5: COMMIT TO A RACE-FIRST LENS

Center the Hardest Problem to Fix Other Problems

Given the persistence and impact of race and racism, we must fully and openly commit to the only antidote there is: antiracism. A race-first lens is the key to enacting an antiracist practice. It positions race as the most important aspect of our identity and therefore of our lived experiences. By using this lens we can articulate clearer questions about the impact race may be having in any situation. *How might interpersonal, institutional, or structural racism be present in this interaction or circumstance? Have I explored a race-first solution to this problem before making a decision? Have I considered how different lived experiences may be informing this moment or situation?*

I BELIEVE RACIAL EQUITY IS THE DEFINING ISSUE OF OUR TIME. THE TRUTH IS, RACE AND RACISM UNEQUIVOCALLY SHAPED THIS COUNTRY, AND BECAUSE OF OUR PAST BEHAVIORS, THEY CONTINUE TO MOLD WHO AND WHERE WE ARE TODAY.

While we're still contending with race for many reasons, I want to focus on three difficult truths about our country that show why a race-first lens is central to your antiracist practice.

We've Never Repaired the Sin of Slavery
Today's problems aren't new. Issues of inequity and inequality can be traced back to the very beginning of the United States: to how this country was colonized, to the slave ships, and to the division of indentured servitude and chattel slavery. The United States was built by stolen people on stolen land; our country, economy, and power were all constructed under a hierarchical and inequitable system.

There's that famous Dr. Maya Angelou quote: "When people show you who they are, believe them." Well, as I mentioned, it took 122 years for the majority-white US government to agree that lynching should be punished as a federal hate crime. That shows me what the majority of many decades' worth of elected officials think of Black people being murdered in a historically anti-Black way. Reparations to descendants of enslaved people have barely made it past initial conversations at the national level. We see the lasting impact of slavery every single day, coupled with anti-Blackness. If you entered into this country in a role of servitude, it seems impossible to get people to cast(e) you in any other role.

THE UNITED STATES HAS APOLOGIZED FOR SLAVERY AND FOR JIM CROW LAWS, BUT ITS PEOPLE STILL HAVEN'T GOTTEN RID OF JIM CROW THINKING.

Black people in the United States, the descendants of enslaved people still live and coexist with the descendants of the people who enslaved and oppressed us. Not only that, but the slave traders erased the history and lineage of the Africans they brought over, so we also do not know our own history. Because of our oppressors, we don't know where we are from; we don't know if we're from Senegal, Ghana, or Nigeria. Even our identities are tied to one of our original oppressors: Black people account for 90 percent of the people with the last name *Washington*.

The relationship between whiteness and Blackness as collective peoples has never been repaired or made whole. Imagine that a friend or partner betrayed you badly, time and time again, for years. When you found out, they apologized but then just moved on. Could *you* truly move on without repairing the hurt and damage that was done? No. Harm hurts, and that hurt doesn't just go away on its own—it takes restoration and trust building, it takes relationships and accountability. Time does not heal all wounds; we need explicit efforts to make up for the harm done before the healing can begin. The South African Truth and Reconciliation Commission, for example, built paths to reparations, rehabilitation, and reconciliation. We can't just pretend that things in the United States are okay because time has passed since this country was built on the uncompensated labor and legal and social oppression of Black people.

Our Collective Barometer of Comfort Is Set to White

In subtle and unsubtle ways, the United States is designed in such a way that everything is set up for white people without them even knowing it. It's like you're driving through life and finding that all the lights are green, there are no pedestrians in the crosswalks, no one cuts you off or swerves into your lane. There are no speed bumps or potholes. Your jams are always playing on the radio. It's smooth sailing.

This manifests in daily life when certain topics are deemed "impolite" because they're not suited for white comfort. It showed up when a white former colleague of mine told me that I "talk about race too much," a comment he made only because *he* didn't want to talk about race and had determined that his comfort was more important than my lived experience. This behavior goes back to the very beginning: facts about brutal and inhumane conditions for enslaved people were erased from Southern history textbooks by the United Daughters of the Confederacy, who heavily influenced textbook and educational decisions.[34] Since then, individuals, organizations, and even the US government have gone to extreme lengths to ensure that critical moments in history are not taught in schools.[35] One friend of mine, a surgeon who has been practicing medicine for more than fifteen years, only recently learned about the Tuskegee Experiment (if you haven't heard of it, look it up). White women can call the police to report BIPOC who are doing nothing illegal, just making the caller uneasy (with activities like bird-watching,[36] loading groceries into a car,[37] or hanging out at a park[38]). The reality is that most white folks don't even know things are set up for them; they just know they had never experienced real discomfort right up to the point they did.

Our Different Lived Experiences Polarize Us

Would you want to be treated the way Black people are treated in this country? Stop now and answer the question.

When asked, most white people will say, if they're answering truthfully, "No." They know that being Black makes it harder to exist in this country. Even if they've only read the whitewashed version of US history, they know that Black people have it worse

---

[34] Greg Huffman, "Twisted Sources: How Confederate propaganda ended up in the South's schoolbooks," *Facing South*, April 10, 2019, https://www.facingsouth.org/2019/04/twisted-sources-how-confederate-propaganda-ended-souths-schoolbooks.

[35] Olivia B. Waxman, "Trump's Threat to Pull Funding From Schools Over How They Teach Slavery Is Part of a Long History of Politicizing American History Class," *Time*, September 16, 2020, https://time.com/5889051/history-curriculum-politics/.

[36] Jan Ransom, "Amy Cooper Faces Charges after Calling Police on Black Bird-Watcher," *New York Times*, July 6, 2020, https://www.nytimes.com/2020/07/06/nyregion/amy-cooper-false-report-charge.html.

[37] Cedric 'BIG CED' Thornton, "White Woman Calls Police On Black Man Placing Groceries In His Car in Ohio," *Black Enterprise*, October 7, 2020, https://www.blackenterprise.com/white-woman-calls-police-on-black-man-placing-groceries-in-his-car-in-ohio/.

[38] Gianluca Mezzofiore, "A white woman called police on black people barbecuing. This is how the community responded," *CNN*, May 22, 2018, https://www.cnn.com/2018/05/22/us/white-woman-black-people-oakland-bbq-trnd/index.html.

than white people. They may not know how badly we have it, but they know that it's not something they want to experience. To me, that ubiquitous no tells us everything about this country: race impacts how we are treated and how we experience day-to-day life. After centuries of this difference, people of different races have different lived experiences.

Do you know how many laws on the books in this country have prevented white folks from doing anything outside of criminal behavior? Not many. I want to highlight three: white women were not allowed to vote until 1920; white folks could not marry people of color until 1967; and LGBTQIA+ marriage equality, for all racial identities, was only federally legalized in 2015. While white folks were able to do nearly anything they ever wanted, federal laws laid many restrictions on people of color. For example, restrictive covenants and redlining made it difficult or impossible for people of color to buy homes. If their skin looked like mine, they were prevented by law from living in particular neighborhoods, and banks could not loan them money.[39]

Stated more directly: white, Black, and brown people experience the world differently and are treated differently out in the world. White people experience entirely different realities than BIPOC, even now. We often live in different communities (the ongoing effect of redlining), so we don't attend the same religious institutions, grow up in the same schools, or shop at the same stores. Because of racial inequity at workplaces, most of us don't work side-by-side with many people of different races, so we don't know just how different their lives are from ours. You won't know until you start listening to and engaging in BIPOC-created stories. And even when you feel like you have a healthy understanding of that, your understanding is very different from their lived reality. But it's okay that you don't know; it's okay not to know everything.

---

39 *Jim Crow of the North* is a good starting point for learning more about restrictive covenants and the practice of redlining.

While this is a Cliff's Notes version of a Cliff's Notes version of only a few details of our historic context and outcomes, I hope these three points capture the depth of where we are at this moment in time. They are not the only reasons we are where we are, but they are significant contributors. I have to state the facts without softening them—we are still dealing with these issues because we have only ever ignored or glossed over them.

These truths show us that race is this country's oldest and most persistent issue. Every social issue or societal challenge we face as a country has a racialized component. For example:

- **Life expectancy:** Non-Hispanic white life expectancy is 77.6 years, whereas it's 71.8 years for non-Hispanic Black people.[40]

- **Violence against women and LGBTQIA+:** The murder rate of American Indian and Alaska Native women is 2.8 times higher than that of non-Hispanic white women.[41] In 2019, 91 percent of transgender and gender-nonconforming individuals murdered in the United States were Black, and in 2018, 82 percent were Black.[42]

- **Poverty rates:** Based on the 2021 and earlier Current Population Survey Annual Social and Economic Supplements (CPS-ASEC) conducted by the US Census Bureau, poverty rates were as follows: non-Hispanic Whites 8.2 percent, Hispanics 17.0 percent, and Blacks 19.5 percent.[43]

---

[40] Elizabeth Arias, Ph.D., Betzaida Tejada-Vera, M.S., Farida Ahmad, M.P.H., and Kenneth D. Kochanek, M.A., "Provisional Life Expectancy Estimates for 2020," *National Vital Statistics System (NVSS)*, Report No. 015, July 2021, https://www.cdc.gov/nchs/data/vsrr/vsrr015-508.pdf.

[41] "Violence Against American Indian and Alaska Native Women," National Congress Of American Indians Policy Research Center, February 2018, https://www.ncai.org/policy-research-center/research-data/prc-publications/VAWA_Data_Brief__FINAL_2_1_2018.pdf.

[42] "A National Epidemic: Fatal Anti-Transgender Violence in the United States in 2019," *Human Rights Campaign*, https://www.hrc.org/resources/a-national-epidemic-fatal-anti-trans-violence-in-the-united-states-in-2019.

[43] Emily A. Shrider, Melissa Kollar, Frances Chen, and Jessica Semega, "Income and Poverty in the United States: 2020," *United States Census Bureau*, https://www.census.gov/library/publications/2021/demo/p60-273.html.

- **Home ownership:** The National Association of Realtors found that in 2020, home ownership rates for white people were 72.1 percent and for Black people 43.3 percent, a 28.8 percent difference.[44]

I could go on and on: rates of literacy and graduation, incarceration, interactions with police and law enforcement, traffic stops, drug addiction, income inequity, reproductive healthcare, healthcare access and treatment, access to financial support (mortgages, business loans, etc.), elected or appointed representation, voting access, maternal mortality, religious persecution, environmental pollution, food access, public transit access, leadership representation, workplace retention, pay equity, and wealth inequity. Statistics about any of these issues when examined by race show that Black and Brown people fare worse. There is not one part of our lived experience that isn't impacted by race.

If you go deeper than statistics, and ask "How did we get here?" about issues that don't *appear* to be about race, you'll find that race is a central component of the answer. Universal healthcare access in the United States may not appear to be a race issue, and yet Heather McGhee outlined in *The Sum of Us: What Racism Costs Everyone and How We Can Prosper Together* that state adoption of the Affordable Care Act was inversely correlated with Black populations. As the percentage of Black population increases, state adoption decreases.[45] McGhee frames it as a zero-sum mindset: White folks are willing to say no to a benefit to ensure that Black folks don't get it either. Public school education funding is another issue shaped by race. Most public schools are funded in part by property taxes. Residents' property tax rates are related to property values—higher values properties have

---

44 Brandi Snowden and Nadia Evangelou, "Racial Disparities in Homeownership Rates," *National Association of Realtors*, March 3, 2020, https://www.nar.realtor/blogs/economists-outlook/racial-disparities-in-homeownership-rates.

45 Heather McGhee, *The Sum of Us: What Racism Costs Everyone and How We Can Prosper Together* (New York: Random House, 2021).

higher property taxes. Redlining and racial covenants led to lower property values in areas that were predominantly Black, and while redlining is no longer legal after the 1968 Fair Housing Act, property values—and therefore school funding—have remained lower in Black and brown neighborhoods ever since. Instead of spreading taxes out evenly across schools, some areas keep more resources than others.

Every facet of the human experience in the United States is worse if you're Black or brown. And because outcomes are always worse when looked at by race, we have to actively center race to get to the root of the problems instead of just treating the symptoms. Centering race is how we finally address this hardest and most persistent unsolved problem. If we don't finally and fully address race, nothing will change. If we approach it head-on, we may be able to make everything else better.

A RACE-FIRST LENS IN ACTION

Committing to and openly centering race in how you perceive and assess the world around you is powerful. It signals a bold commitment to acknowledging the ongoing presence and harm of racism. It also signals a commitment to changing yourself, your sphere of influence, and the society around you in order to eliminate racism. It communicates that you want to reorganize the systems and structures that perpetuate our racist history.

We must bring race into our daily actions and behaviors in a more productive and effective way. Race-first framing is a robust tool for adopting a more aware and analytical perspective on the intersection of race and the circumstances around us every day. And it's simple to do: form a new lens by adding *race* to whatever topic or situation is in front of you. For example:

- Race + job requirements
- Race + compensation

- Race + recruitment and hiring at work
- Race + retention at work
- Race + work projects and assignments
- Race + client/customer-engaging (not just customer-facing) activities
- Race + performance reviews
- Race + leadership skills

Introducing race first generates questions around the topics, including:

- Have we examined our requirements alongside the actual job responsibilities to determine how we might be perpetuating implicit bias? For example, is a college degree or x number of years experience actually necessary?
- How may race have impacted a candidate's previous compensation, thereby rendering it inequitable, and how does that inform the salary you might offer?
- How racially diverse is our candidate pool? How are we ensuring a more racially diverse pool?
- What is the data for retention in our company based on race?
- How does race determine who works on important projects and in the most important roles?
- How does race determine who engages in more-involved client interactions?
- What impact does race have on annual reviews? What data are you gathering from BIPOC about their employee experience during these reviews?

- How does race impact people differently in annual reviews?

- Does race change how we perceive leaders and the characteristics that they exhibit?

When you don't center race in your accompliceship, here's how it plays out: You say you care about women's rights and want to fight for women's pay equity. You gather women together to form a coalition and host a series of meetings. Those meeting rooms are filled with women having great conversations, talking passionately, and pushing and championing each other. Yet because you left out a race perspective, you may end up with an all white coalition trying to solve a problem that BIPOC women have always experienced far more acutely.

Black women were the first women in the US workforce; enslaved Black women worked long hours in indigo, rice, tobacco, and cotton fields. They were raped by their owners to produce children to replenish the enslaved labor force. As Deborah Gray White wrote in *Ar'n't I a Woman*, "Once slaveholders realized that the reproductive function of the female slave could yield a profit, the manipulation of procreative sexual relations became an integral part of the sexual exploitation of female slaves."[46] The women then had to bear, feed, and rear those children in addition to any of their own, and to nurse the enslavers' children from their own bodies if white women wanted a wet nurse. So, if you're talking about work and pay equity without an intersectional group of women (specifically including Black women), what are you even doing? What kind of impact can you make? If white women alone could have solved pay equity, it would be solved. It sounds harsh, but our best intentions are flawed when we don't center the issues or problems with the greatest impact.

Two short client stories come to mind about the damage DEIAA work without a race-first lens can inflict. The first was a financial

---

[46] I use the term *enslaved people*, but I reproduce White's writing here. Deborah Gray White, *Ar'n't I a Woman? Female Slaves in the Plantation South*, (New York: W. W. Norton & Company, 1999).

services company that was increasing representation of BIPOC in their promotional materials to demonstrate that BIPOC were welcome at their institutions. In addition to ads, they created an email campaign for home financing that featured an image of a Black woman who was about thirty-five years old. The copy read, "Have poor credit? We can help. No matter your credit history, we offer low-interest loans." As the only person in this picture, this Black woman becomes a representation for perceived irresponsible behaviors and bad decisions that often lead to bad credit. The second was a retail store that created a multipage mailer for the holidays—think smiling families and kids in red sweaters opening presents as snow falls in the background. The store was also aiming to increase representation in their materials by featuring models of different ages, with disabilities, in same-sex relationships, and so on. The last page showed a Black woman with two kids. No partner was in the literal picture, so I'm guessing she was supposed to represent the millions of single-parent households in our country. While you might think that these are extreme links to make, if we push these stereotypes forward, we perpetuate our inability to see people as fully human. Are there Black women who need access to low-barrier financing due to poor credit? Of course. Are there single Black mothers? Of course. But if that is the *only* way Black women are represented, it can be interpreted as playing off stereotypes rather than a genuine attempt at inclusion. On the other end of these campaigns, the real people who identify with the individuals represented, who see the ads or who work at those companies, are reminded that systemic racism reduces them to a stereotype.

If the advertising teams had applied a race-first lens to those ads, they would have asked questions like, *How does this representation relate to the history of Blackness and racial identities in this country? What is this picture telling the viewer about race and the racialized individuals in it? How might people who racially identify with the person in the ad feel about this representation?*

IT'S NOT THAT YOU CAN'T DO ANY GOOD WITHOUT CENTERING RACE, BUT YOU WILL DO THE MOST GOOD WHEN YOU ASK QUESTIONS ROOTED IN OUR RACIAL HISTORY.

Intersectionality Is a Must

Kimberlé Williams Crenshaw coined the term *intersectionality* to address how some social justice problems, like racism and sexism, overlap and create compounding levels of injustice. The Oxford Languages dictionary defines the term as "the interconnected nature of social categorizations such as race, class, and gender as they apply to a given individual or group, regarded as creating overlapping and interdependent systems of discrimination or disadvantage."

As Crenshaw states, "Intersectionality is just a metaphor for understanding the ways that multiple forms of inequality or disadvantage sometimes compound themselves, and they create obstacles that often are not understood within conventional ways of thinking about anti-racism or feminism or whatever social justice advocacy structures we have. Intersectionality isn't so much a grand theory, it's a prism for understanding certain kinds of problems. African-American girls are six times more likely to be suspended than white girls. That's probably a race and a gender problem; it's not just a race problem, it's not just a gender problem."

Intersectionality can teach accomplices that, in every circumstance in our daily lives and work, there may be multiple identities overlapping and affecting individuals or groups in unique, exponential ways. So yes, I want you to commit to using a race-first lens, but after you've centered race, I always want you to also think more broadly so you're understanding, as much as you can, how multiple aspects of who people are inform the situations you're in. Gender, sexual and gender identity, citizenship status, ability–among other identity markers–all play into how a person might be doubly or triply impacted by systems and structures that were designed for dominant identities.

WHAT A RACE-FIRST LENS CAN GET YOU

The beauty of new questions based on race and an antiracist practice is that they allow you to have new conversations. Right now, we are in the scariest place I've seen in a long time in this country. Effective conversations that center race are our way out. The world is becoming more diverse, and within a decade, the ability to have conversations about race and racialized lived experiences will be a required skill. The more conversations you have, the better you will get at having them. The bonus is that talking effectively and openly about race will help you handle every other difficult topic much more comfortably and fluently because you've already had the hardest conversation.

In your workplace, centering race might show up as asking race-based questions when there is conflict on a team. Or it might show up as vulnerably asking your all-white team to have an honest discussion about why there are not more BIPOC in their networks or how race might be playing into their business decisions. Ignoring your personal awareness of race and neglecting to bring it into conversations at work will have consequences. Remember the leadership team in the first chapter, the ones who had all kinds of diversity goals but could not discuss their own race? That company is having a brain drain of BIPOC employees right now. Leadership went all-in on hiring to achieve a quota and gave up on the self-work, but because they didn't have those conversations, they failed to adequately promote, compensate, and engage with their BIPOC employees. Then, the person they hired to lead the DEIAA efforts (because they didn't want to do the work) left the position after barely getting started.

"So, Seena, what should I do?" I'm so glad you asked. Conversations about race and racial equity don't have to be dramatic confrontations. Start with your truth and your perspective on what's going on. You don't need to take anyone or any ideology down in order to share what you believe as a leader and as a company. You also don't need to walk up to your Black and brown employees and ask them direct questions about their race. When I guide my clients in conversations about race and racism, I share four specific to-dos.

Share your perspective on race and racial equity.
Do you value equity? If so, state it and share why. Do you think race impacts our lives? Share that. You don't need an academic or rigorous position; the point is to open the door to words that are usually not used at work. By demonstrating that race, racialized experiences, and equity are topics you think and care about as a leader, you also indicate that these are worthwhile and valuable topics.

Make space for people to share their truth and bring their full selves to conversations about their experiences, especially if they have a skin experience that is not white.
Employee resource groups and affinity groups can offer safe spaces for individuals to have effective conversations about their work experience with people who share their identity. Another option is to host conversations led by a third-party facilitator to examine what people are thinking, what they are feeling, and what they need.

Listen carefully when people speak up or share.
This is the time to take in information that people are sharing, not to argue, discuss, or push back. When BIPOC and other historically underrepresented people share their experiences, they are not lying. If they are opening up to you, it is your opportunity to truly be an

accomplice and practice awareness (What are they telling me, and what am I learning?), analysis (How does this information change our situation?), and action (see below).

Move to action in some way around what they share.
Ask very directly, "How can I support you?" Then, to the greatest degree possible, provide that support. If you can't, circle back and share why. Purposefully investigate avenues for integrating their feedback into the work environment. If you fail to take action on what they tell you, even unintentionally, you send the message that you don't have their back.

I was having a one-on-one session with my client Gabe on Monday, April 19, 2021. The Derek Chauvin trial had recently come to an end, and we knew the verdict was going to be read soon. Gabe, a white man, works at a Fortune 1000 company and leads a team of about 150 people mostly based in the Twin Cities area. At the time, he was new to our program but had been very present and committed during the first few months.

"What do you think is most important at this moment?" I asked him.

He answered, "I want everyone to know I support whatever they have to do for themselves given whatever verdict is read. I'm nervous that I will come across as telling people how to process. Yet, I know I want to say something beforehand. I don't want anyone on my team having to reach out to me to explain their case." He paused, then went on, "I know I didn't really answer your question. I guess I just don't know how to bring it up."

I replied, "It's important that you unequivocally state your position on race and racial equity as it pertains to this moment. As a leader, it's first and foremost your role to set the tone and guardrails for what is considered appropriate to discuss on your team. If you say the words *race* and *racial equity*, then others implicitly understand that it's permissible for them to bring up the topics too. You can also say that you want to make space for every single team member to bring their full selves to work and acknowledge that that will mean a unique thing to every person. That signals to your colleagues that you welcome their individuality and individual lived experience. And then simply ask them how you can support them. Be proactive and available, as you would for a friend or family member who is going through a tough time."

In instances like these, tell your BIPOC employees that they can go home, tell them that they can process the events however they need to, tell them that at the end of the day, they don't need to share or talk about any of this with anyone if they don't want to. That is how to apply a race-first lens; consider what BIPOC, and in this case Black folks specifically, may need to hear at any given moment. Gabe didn't need a speech or a proclamation, but you do need to engage in consistent conversations that demonstrate racial awareness. And in these instances, so do you.

We won't solve racism overnight, but a race-first lens will expand your awareness and problem-solving capacity to include race like never before. It's a critical way to engage in antiracist thinking and to actively work against racism's multidimensional, and often covert, aspects.

PAUSE FOR AWARENESS AND ANALYSIS

- What do you know now that you didn't know before?
- Do you believe you have what it takes to develop a race-first lens?
- Does it make you nervous, anxious, or uncomfortable to consider race in your decision-making?
- Does it make you uncomfortable to say, "I'm antiracist?"
- Would it make you uncomfortable to use the word *antiracist* in your mission, vision, values, or promotional materials?
- What support, information, or resources do you need to truly possess and apply a race first lens in your workplace?
- After reading this chapter, what might you need a moment to sit with and further unpack?

MOVE TO ACTION

Create a Brave Space at Your Workplace

Have you heard the term *safe space*? It's commonly used to establish a setting in which people feel like they can be authentic and honest with no judgment. In theory that's very positive. In practice it can be something else, a space in which all kinds of things are irresponsibly shared under the guise of feeling "safe" or "speaking my truth." That raises questions like *Safe for who? Who sets the parameters? Who's in control? Where is the power in the space? Who can safely share their truths and be their full selves?*

A brave space has no judgment, but unlike safe spaces, it also has accountability. That accountability aspect is key; accountability means that you are responsible if you make an *oops* or cause an *ouch*. A safe space presumes equality; a brave space promotes equity. I find that this slight twist on showing up in spaces sets the stage for more effective participation and culture building. In brave spaces, individuals have to listen and engage with more attention to others. In brave spaces, impact is more important than intention.

Creating brave spaces is one of the most effective ways that you as a leader can move your organization toward equity. Perhaps you have data from staff surveys or exit interviews; make space for individuals to share with you directly, too. Ask frequently: *How can I support you? What other support might you need? Are there things you need that you do not have?* Maybe they need time, different equipment, or something you've never even imagined!

To create brave spaces, define what it means: All individuals (including yourself) will be held accountable for any missteps. State that in brave spaces, we listen and take action based on what we learn. Consider other qualities of what *brave* may mean for your environment and be open and clear about those conditions.

When you create truly brave spaces where people feel safe, people will share their experiences. They will tell you what's wrong and often what could fix these wrongs as well. It's not rocket science, but it takes an active, intentional creation of space.

CHAPTER 6: ACKNOWLEDGE YOUR RACIAL IDENTITY

Who We Are Isn't Always as Simple as It Seems

Because our racial identities shape our lived experiences and the situations in which we find ourselves, it is crucial that we understand our own race and racial identity, and what those mean in any given context. If you are a business owner, CEO, or team leader but have never thought about your own racial identity or what impact your race might have on the people you lead and manage, it can be more difficult for you to excel in your role. Not thinking about your own and others' racial identities as you navigate leadership waters puts you at a disadvantage: You are omitting a significant amount of data on interpersonal dynamics, personal behaviors, and individual needs, and thus you are operating with a limited understanding.

As we encounter other people, we often make assessments and judgments based on how they appear. In other words, we racialize people. Put simply, to racialize is to categorize or divide people according to race. When I walk out of my front door, other people register my Blackness before they see or assume that I'm a woman, neighbor, Twin Citian, college grad, parent, and fantastic dresser! My husband is Ghanaian, but he is not identified as such by others; to most people, he is a Black man. And white folks are white, not Irish or Scandinavian. So ethnicity and other attributes take a back seat to whatever our skin looks like.

Racialization is not always conscious. And it's not always damaging and limiting, though it very often is.

I BELIEVE RACE IS THE SEAT OF OUR BIASES AND ASSUMPTIONS, WHICH PLAY OUT IN SMALL AND SIGNIFICANT WAYS IN OUR RELATIONSHIPS AND INTERACTIONS.

Before we continue, I want to go on record: We all have biases and make assumptions. Everyone—no matter how good an "I don't see differences" game they talk—moves through the world with biases. These biases make room for outcomes ranging from arbitrary to interesting to dangerous. For example, comments like "You don't look like a lawyer" rely on a very specific assumption about who lawyers are and what they look like. It's imperative that we don't ignore race when we think about who we are and where we are today as a culture, and how our own identities and behaviors are influenced by our race and racialized experiences.

Racializing people is part of the water we swim in, which is why it is dangerous to say "I don't see race" or "Race isn't contributing to how I'm thinking about this." Because you do and it is, and it is a lived reality for all BIPOC. Examining our biases and assumptions is such an important step in changing our collective circumstance: If people can see how their conversations and interactions are skewed by their biases and assumptions, they can start to question what they're bringing to their interactions and why. A key behavior for an accomplice is questioning why things are the way they are and then following your line of investigation as deeply and thoroughly as you can.

How do *you* racially identify, and why do you identify that way? How often do you feel that your race impedes your progress or success? I really want you to sit and think about this.

I ask these questions because white people have rarely, if ever, had to think about their race. In session after session I observe that, when asked, white people often have a hard time naming their whiteness as a primary part of their identity, and they get even more uncomfortable describing why they identify that way. The number-one thing I hear is that white people have rarely had to think about their race, let alone consciously process the implications of that racial identity in various spaces and with various people. They've never been restricted from doing something because of their race or treated as less - than because of their race. Moving through the world without having to think about their own race means that it's hard to all of a sudden contend with it. White people are always supposed to be comfortable, and talking about race challenges that comfort. So white comfort has kept us all from engaging in critical conversations about race.

Being Black, Indigenous, or Hispanic in a room means something different than being white because race is a social construct built on hierarchy. How much metaphorical space we take up is influenced by our identity and what society has taught us about that identity. Some people speak only when spoken to; others feel entitled to speak freely and at length regardless of who is interested. Whether you have ever considered this or not, what we opine on and when we keep our mouths shut are informed by our racialized experiences. Where are you in your understanding of how your race might shape the way you take up and share space in conversation? Do you observe who is or is not sharing in group conversations? Do you demonstrate appreciation when someone shares a perspective that may run counter to the dominant culture's expectations? These are critical considerations, and not because people from historically excluded groups have a woe-is-me or a woe-is-us mindset. It's simply that we are all products of socialization, racialization, and conditioning, and those histories and experiences play out in every situation.

As individuals in my cohorts share their responses to the question "How do you racially identify, and why do you identify that way?" white people start to observe that race impacts the majority of BIPOC lived experience: how they're treated, how they're required to show up, and how they navigate the unwritten social contracts we all deal with. There is a slow realization that they have whiteness, that a lot of privilege comes with it, and part of that privilege is that they never have to think about their racial identity.

I also see people feeling guilt and shame about the fact that they've never thought about it. This conversation and reckoning are new territory. Most of them are grown adults who are good at their jobs, they're brilliant about coding, nonprofit management, or marketing and branding. They've developed a set of skills to pursue success in their professional paths. But they don't know about racial identity because they've never talked about it. And that's when they start to feel deficient.

I want to share a story that illustrates how much of a disadvantage you may be at without an awareness of your race and its historical context and others'. My client Sheila was part of a large company in the beauty industry; she was an instructor and often worked closely with students who were learning the industry trade. In one of our sessions, Sheila processed a difficult exchange with a group of BIPOC students who had requested that they be taught textured hair lessons from a person of color. Sheila was white, so that also meant, implicitly, that they were asking her *not* to be their instructor for the textured hair lessons. She was very frustrated and offended by the request because she was an accomplished and experienced stylist and instructor who had worked for decades on all types of hair. Her students' request felt very personal to her. Her reactions included, "I know what I'm doing!" and, "I'm a great teacher, and I don't see why I should not engage in that part of the work just because they want a specific type of teacher." Now, I don't doubt that Sheila could work on textured hair, but that wasn't really the point.

She wasn't thinking about how her race and that of her students informed the situation. She struggled with the request because she only saw it within the narrow context of "the students don't think I can teach them about textured hair." In contrast, the BIPOC students were likely coming from a racialized set of lived experiences and understood that learning from someone who shared their common hair experience—and the experience of future customers—would be a richer, more personalized educational opportunity.

That right there is what Sheila was missing when she didn't examine her own race; this wasn't about *her*, it was about the racial dynamics at play. Had she stepped back and acknowledged how her whiteness shaped the students' experience, she might have seen their request differently. Acknowledging your race and its role in your interactions and experiences allows you to move past *you* and to instead consider the power, hierarchy, and systems that operate in the background of every situation. Our racial differences are not always as clearly on display as they were in Sheila's story; you can imagine how differences could be exponentially more possible to misinterpret in a subtler circumstance.

In today's business world, leadership requires more than intellect or industry knowledge. Effective leadership also requires a deep understanding of people and emotional intelligence around what they experience as individuals. Leaders spend time understanding work styles, individual strengths, and group dynamics to help propel their teams and business forward. Organizations even administer assessments, such as StrengthsFinder, to better understand how to maximize individual contributions, or they create deeply detailed performance plans to ensure team members are achieving goals. Leaders take part in these activities to help their colleagues be their best at work and to create the strongest organization they can. If you're a leader or manager who does any of that, you should also be considering how race contributes to individuals' behaviors, experiences, and performance at work. You should be aware that asking, "So how did everyone celebrate the great spring weather this weekend?!" at the Monday staff meeting might feel very insensitive to BIPOC who know that the weekend marked the first anniversary of Breonna Taylor's death. Asking people's favorite road-trip destinations as an icebreaker at a workshop ignores the fact that BIPOC have never been afforded the comfort of getting in their cars and driving through remote rural areas without an element of fear. Some of the most basic activities—like antiquing in shops filled with little racist figurines—can result in very different lived experiences for BIPOC. While people can be solely defined by their racial identity, it benefits all of us to pay more attention to how our racial identities affect our lived experience. I'm not saying that you can't enjoy your life and be happy about your experiences, but it's important to have the awareness that not everyone has the same experiences and to act accordingly.

The Price Black People Pay

One thing Black people know is that if we're going to succeed at anything, we've got to smash all the records. We can't just get a bronze medal; no one cares about the bronze. We have to be Allyson Felix, right? We have to get the gold. That's Black tax: having to work two or three times as much to get less credit and less compensation than our white peers.

Black tax can prevent us from getting into an organization or a preferred role in it. Even when we have reached a high level, the tax doesn't go away. It increases. Couple that with the emotional labor of often being one of only a few Black people (the only one), we have additional labor on top of our tax. Here's a quote from the 2020 Lean In study *The State of Black Women in Corporate America*: "I feel like expectations for me as a Black woman are much higher than those of my white counterparts. It feels like I am expected to go above and beyond while my colleagues at the same level just do what is described in our job descriptions." Another respondent said, "I feel like I have to represent the entire race. I need to come across as more than proficient, more than competent, more than capable. I have to be 'on' all the time. Because in the back of someone's mind, they could be judging the entire race based on me."[47]

On any given day in the workplace; the number of things Black people manage in addition to their actual job duties is high. A study by Catalyst, a global nonprofit, found:

"Specifically, our data show that the Emotional Tax [another term for Black tax] can deplete Black employees' sense of well-being by making them feel that they have to be 'on guard,' disrupting sleep patterns, reducing their sense of 'psychological safety,' and diminishing their ability to contribute at work."[48]

That presentation we're asked to do? We know it has to be perfect. That time a client assumes we're the secretary, not the VP? We know why they assumed that. That time we had to call out the senior VP for saying something casually racist? We know that we're possibly being labeled "difficult" or "confrontational." Because Black people have to have enough hands to hold all this, we just be ourselves. And, ironically, it makes it harder to get our actual work done because we're already so overtaxed.

Last year, in our initial culture assessment survey with a new client organization, BIPOC employees reported that their white boss scheduled a meeting with BIPOC staff early in the morning on the Sunday (yes, Sunday) the week after George Floyd was murdered in hopes of having the BIPOC employees help him draft a company

---

[47] *The State of Black Women in Corporate America 2020*, Lean In, accessed July 29, 2022, https://leanin.org/research/state-of-black-women-in-corporate-america.

[48] *Emotional Tax: How Black Women and Men Pay More at Work and How Leaders Can Take Action*, Catalyst, accessed July 29, 2022, https://www.catalyst.org/wp-content/uploads/2019/01/emotional_tax_how_black_women_and_men_pay_more.pdf.

statement about the murder—like he had seen many other companies doing. (I suspect I was hired to help address that very incident.) You can imagine that what it meant for a white person to make that request was very different than if BIPOC had initiated it themselves or if a Black leader had initiated a conversation. Our racialized differences inevitably contribute to our interactions in moments as charged as these, but they do so every day in short interactions as well:

- Who gets attention and what kind of attention they receive.

- Who does not receive attention or slides under the radar.

- Who is asked to help out in what type of situations.

- How people support others throughout an organization.

- Who can speak to and about circumstances.

As a leader, do you work as intentionally with your BIPOC employees on their career paths and planning as you do with white employees? Are you promoting employees of different races at the same rates? Do you ask Black employees to lead employee resource groups without additional resources, compensation, or consideration for their existing roles and related responsibilities? Are you over reliant on white employees to help you write diversity and inclusion statements for your website?

Acknowledging your how racial identity and how it contributes to the way you move through the world and understand the people around you will help you observe more about race and all of its complexities. In many countries, including the United States, proximity to whiteness is preferred. Black is wrong, white is right. So if you are white identified or have lighter skin, it is important to acknowledge that your racial identity comes with privilege that other people are not given. Now here's where I say that if you're a white person, I don't want you to feel guilt or shame around that. None of us got to choose! I want you to feel unafraid to name your own racial identity—it's not an exit ramp from accompliceship, it's a gateway to it.

MICROAGGRESSIONS

If we're not attentive to our own race, the implications of racializing in our country, and the biases that are based on racialization, we can commit microaggressions, a term coined by Dr. Chester M. Pierce, a Harvard professor. According to Dr. Kevin Nadal, "Microaggressions are defined as the everyday, subtle, intentional—and oftentimes unintentional—interactions or behaviors that communicate some sort of bias toward historically underrepresented groups. The difference between microaggressions and overt discrimination (or macroaggressions), is that people who commit microaggressions might not even be aware of them."[49] When I was in graduate school, I once told a Chinese classmate that her English had gotten so much better over the course of the semester. That is an example of a microaggression (and proof that we all make mistakes in this work). I presumed that speaking English with less of an accent was "better." It is not, and I cannot imagine how she felt hearing that and thinking back on her past self whose English wasn't as "good."

Microaggressions have been described as death by one thousand papercuts. And that is one reason they can be so challenging. Each microaggression on its own isn't a big deal, but when you experience them repeatedly, they have an enormous effect. As in the textured hair teaching story above, we can miss the racial significance of something entirely if we don't ask ourselves, "How might race, mine or someone else's, be affecting this situation? Is there something I am missing by not thinking about race as it applies to this moment?"

---

[49] Andrew Limbong, "Microaggressions are a big deal: How to talk them out and when to walk away," *NPR.com*, June 9, 2020, https://www.npr.org/2020/06/08/872371063/microaggressions-are-a-big-deal-how-to-talk-them-out-and-when-to-walk-away.

And microaggressions are definitely happening. A 2021 study by Savanta, a market research company, found that three in four BIPOC had experienced microaggressions at work in the past year and 84 percent of BIPOC had experienced discrimination of some kind in the past year.[50] And those experiences were in a post-George Floyd world, so people *knew* better.

Here are a few examples of microaggressions. If you want to know more, there are many articles and firsthand accounts of these experiences online.

- Saying to a Black person, "You're so articulate. You speak really well."

- Asking, "Where are you *really* from?" of a Hispanic, Asian, or brown person.

- Tone policing a Black person by asking, "Why are you getting so angry?" when a racist or inequitable situation arises at work.

- Saying, "How's everything going, Kim?" when the person you're speaking to is Sonja, the other Black woman at the office.

- Asking to shorten, or shortening without consent, a person's name to a letter or a more Western-sounding nickname instead of saying their full name.

- Touching or asking to touch someone's hair. For the record, never do this.

I recommend doing a deep dive into accounts and examples of microaggressions because they are happening everywhere, all of the time, and waiting for a colleague or employee to raise the issue puts the onus on them. Anyone and everyone can witness microaggressions if they pay attention.

---

[50] "Black Lives Matter: Everywhere," *Savanta*, January 2021, accessed July 29, 2022, https://info.savanta.com/hubfs/BLM%20report/Savanta%20BLM%20Everywhere%20-%20report%20FINAL2.pdf.

Then, if someone at work *does* say they experienced a microaggression, believe them. I promise that it is taking a lot of guts for them to share it, and they might have ignored or downplayed many other offenses up until that moment. When they share, even if it does not feel to you like it rises to the occasion of "offense" or "aggression," believe that it does because it is undoubtedly an accumulation of experiences.

Leaders who address a single instance, even if it doesn't feel significant, can make a difference. When you address "small" instances—again, the impacts of these incidents are not as small as they may seem—you establish healthy practices. This creates a culture of naming things. Addressing a comment or an incident doesn't mean you have to blow a gasket or go on the offensive. You can simply name what happened and share your perspective on it. Like, "That kind of language isn't acceptable. Please don't use it." Addressing moments as they happen is also the path toward incremental change on your team. Just like we can't deconstruct racism in one broad stroke, you can't instill a culture of antiracism with a single big statement or grand gesture. Antiracism is practiced in everyday moments, like naming things that are repeatedly and consistently done. Then, when you take action after hearing from a colleague, you show people that you support them. If you dismiss their experience or excuse others' behaviors, it likewise sends a clear message about what and whom you care about.

If we're going to meet aggressive goals as teammates in our workplaces, we have to be able to be our whole selves, speak our truth, and contend with the work at hand. Microaggressions prevent BIPOC from full engagement. But once you've done your own learning around race and racial identity, you can more easily understand others—you can't live their experience in the workplace, but you can be open to learning from it. This allows for greater connection and better chances of working productively and effectively together. When everyone is more in tune with how their race and racialization affect the circumstances around them, more honest conversations and interactions, and hopefully all the brightest ideas, can unfold.

PAUSE FOR AWARENESS AND ANALYSIS

- What do you know now that you didn't know before?
- How does your racial identity impact your everyday life?
- Is this the first time you've consciously thought about your racial identity?
- How might your biases come into play when thinking about the racial identity of others?
- Do you understand what your racial identity represents in the racialized US system, and could you speak to it if someone asked you?

MOVE TO ACTION

Examine Your Biases and Assumptions

If you're aspiring to be an accomplice, don't rest on the laurels of recognizing that you have biases and make assumptions. Fervently contend with and unpack the biases and understand how you can use them to create better situations and circumstances. The point isn't to fight them—it's to examine them.

Our individual biases are a way to solve our collective problems. Biases and assumptions are rooted in stereotypes, and the reality is that no group is a monolith. Whatever stereotype you base your assumptions on will be incorrect for some of the folks within that group. If you as a leader are making policies or decisions based on assumptions rooted in inaccurate stereotypes, you will end up with harmful policies and decisions. The danger in unexamined biases and assumptions is plentiful:

- You'll miss out on the top talent because you or your HR team overlook candidates based on unchecked biases or algorithmic racial bias that filters out the resumes of certain candidates.

- You'll miss out on the best ideas because you believe that you, or your team, know who should be in the room for brainstorming.

- It puts you further out of touch with potential clients or constituents because you allow stereotypes or generalizations to cloud your decisions.

- It makes you a poor colleague because you don't allow the people around you to be individuals.

- It makes you a horrible accomplice.

You can Google an article on how to examine your biases and assumptions, but overall, I think people should pause more. Move through the world with more intentionality: Observe your thoughts, notice your reactions to people around you, and recognize how others respond to you. But more than anything, question yourself and your actions. When you notice yourself acting with bias or making assumptions, ask:

- Where did that thought originate?
- Why do I think that?
- Is that true? Am I sure?

Most importantly, notice when you're wrong. Add that to your well of information, which will hopefully fill up over time to more conscientiously, and intentionally, offer a counterargument to your biases and assumptions.

Also, don't @ me if you've done unconscious bias training and think that means you are now unbiased. That is not the case. Period.

CHAPTER 7: DEFINE WHAT YOU'RE WILLING TO WORK FOR

This Isn't Just Head Work; It's Heart Work

Of course, we are all more complex than how we present racially—we're whole people, *you're* a whole person. A person who cares about a lot of things, like maybe dogs, contemporary art, or horror movies. A person who is motivated by their kids or dedicated to a cause, or who wants to leave the world a little better than they found it. Who you are can intersect with what you now know about race to push you further and deeper into engaging as an accomplice. In fact, who you are, what you care about, and what drives you *should* intersect with your journey.

What's in your heart—the things that most deeply affect you on an emotional level—is how you can make a difference in the face of such a large, overwhelming, and persistent issue as race. Imagine a huge boulder the size of the state of California. No one person could move something that large. Heck, thousands of people couldn't move it if they only tried pushing it, hoping it would roll away. But, if every person consistently chipped away at a portion of the boulder, diligently doing their small part each day, eventually the boulder would start to crumble. My point: we don't all have to do everything, but we each have to do something. And this chapter is all about finding the personal inroads to help your head and heart opt in every day.

As you may remember, being an accomplice is not a skill set; it's a practice to help you move through the world, make decisions, understand your situations and surroundings, and interact with people more effectively and empathetically. A practice is self-driven. You don't need someone to tell you how to drive less if you're practicing an eco-focused life—you just make certain decisions that fulfill your commitment. You don't need someone to remind you to recycle or consider your carbon footprint if you care about the environment because that is a natural part of how you behave. So yes, there is an important and urgent reason why you should be an accomplice: We exist in an inequitable world that unfairly impacts BIPOC, and we need to solve the issue of race in order to solve any other issue. But there is also a smaller, more personal and intimate *why* that motivates you. And that is how you adopt and continuously opt in to an antiracist practice.

If you're committed to a practice, opting in and enacting it every day is essential. You're not a vegetarian if you only omit meat from your diet one day a week or only at lunch. We see a lot of occasional engagement when it comes to antiracism. After George Floyd was murdered, did you pay more attention to other news stories about police violence? As hate crimes against Asians were rising around the country during COVID, did you donate money to Stop AAPI Hate, an organization formed in 2020 to raise awareness of the crimes being committed against Asian American and Pacific Islander communities? The truth is, when something notable, and often violent or negative, happens, people pay attention. Then the news cycles move on, and so does the attention. As a Black woman, I find it incredibly frustrating and saddening that white folks only seem to pay attention to our community when something horrific happens. The endless posting of sentiments or the sharing of violent deaths on social media is exhausting. In those moments it can feel like folks are being performative at the expense of people's grief. The kicker is that this action (even the performative displays) is too often relegated to the moments when the shit hits the fan. We need folks to think about racial equity constantly and move to action daily so that we don't have to grieve over and over and wonder whether *this* instance will get white folks to fully opt in.

Yes, major acts of violence or inequity need our attention, but there are moments every day in which you can be putting your accompliceship to work—like my Zoom-bomb moment or the casual microaggressions in the workplace kitchen. They aren't huge or newsworthy, but they are real for the individuals involved. You will only take action in those moments if you're ready, confident that you can do something with your power and privilege. That's the practice.

I have noticed that white people often opt in to the fight against racism only when their lived experience is impacted by race; this is when they start to really care on a heart level. People may be personally affected when a person of color enters into their family, when their child partners with or marries a person who is not white. Suddenly, they have an intimate connection to a person who is racialized differently than them and has lived experiences very different from their white family members. This really wakes people up. They start thinking about traffic stops differently when they read data showing that Black drivers are more likely to be pulled over by police than white drivers and realize that their new relative may have direct experience of it.

We often care more about things that affect us or people we care about. That's very human. Things that are close to us—our hearts, our experiences, our interests—feel more accessible. The more you can put yourself into this work, the better you will be at it. What do I mean by that?

IDENTIFYING WHAT YOU'RE WILLING TO WORK FOR WILL BETTER EQUIP YOU TO SUPPORT OTHER PEOPLE.

It goes back to the premise of awareness: a deep understanding of who we are will help us understand and assist others in the work. If we know how we stay motivated, how we best focus our energy and attention, and how we can most personally move to action, we are more likely to stay engaged. There will never be a scenario in which a BIPOC leader says, "Do this [antiracist thing] to make the world better!" and then you do it, and then they tell you to do another thing and you do it. That is not what we mean by "follow BIPOC." It's much less literal than that. You will never get a checklist of actions or a set of orders (issuing those is emotional labor). You will learn from what you hear, observe, and absorb on your journey, but staying motivated to consistently move to action is on you.

Your why and your lane define what you're willing to work for because they highlight what you care about. Your why is your internal motivation. It will cut right to your heart and connect you deeply to the work. It's how you will opt in every day. Your lane is a set of interests that you already care about and that are already a part of your life. Your lane is how you will narrow your focus and maintain your attention.

Your Why

- A core motivation that fuels your engagement with the broader world and aligns with your purpose.

- Examples: I want to leave the world better than how I found it. I want all people to have bodily independence.

Your Lane

- A set of interests that represents what you care about; extrinsic expressions of who you are.

- Examples: education, outdoors, policy making, neighborhood development, software design, pay equity.

Together, your why and your lane are your intentional areas of focus that are deeply part of who you are. They will shape what you're willing to work for. By connecting your practice to these aspects of your head and heart, you will become a fiercer and more dedicated accomplice.

WHAT'S YOUR WHY?

Our why keeps us going when things feel uncomfortable, when we are frustrated, when things take more effort than we wish to give, and when we feel sad about the state of the world. I feel sad all of the time that we're still fighting fights that I was fighting in 2000, let alone in the 1960s or earlier. Sometimes I am sad that I have an entire career built on educating people about how to fix this ugly, invasive thing called racism. But I know my why: I engage in the work of antiracism because I know what happened to my ancestors. I know how hard they worked, the racism they faced, the moments of joy that they found, and the battles they fought. I wake up every day thinking about how I can make them proud, make their suffering mean something bigger, build on their accomplishments, and help them rest more easily wherever they are now. All of my business decisions align with that passion. I am willing to say no to a client if I don't think that work would give my grandmother something positive to talk about. I prioritize my business decisions around what the generations before me would have done if they'd had the opportunity or what they would want me to do in this time and place. All of my actions come from this place; they are what I'm willing to work for. I am willing to risk everything to give my ancestors closure. I don't even have to think about it.

What motivates you? What internal drive or passion do you find yourself going back to over and over again such that it feels entirely integral or central to who you are?

As you may have noticed, my why isn't explicitly about work, but it informs and influences how I show up and what I show up for in my professional life. Our internal motivations should positively transcend our job or company. This bigger-than-me drive helps you stay focused when the work before you feels hard or disheartening—and that is exactly why it is so important to identify it. This work—chipping away at our systemic problems—isn't always easy and doesn't always feel good. You will be going against the strong headwind of "the way things are," and being able to pick your head up and focus on something farther out, bigger than that moment, will keep you going forward.

FIND YOUR LANE

As you begin to engage with the world as an accomplice, it's important to determine the exact things you care about because there is just too damn much for any one person to do without narrowing things down a little. If you can't access something, or if something in the work doesn't resonate with you, you will rarely move to action. For example, a friend once took me to a nonprofit animal hospital. I thoroughly enjoyed the visit, but I knew I couldn't commit to becoming intimately involved with the organization. I personally would never be self-motivated to stay opted in to animal rights. I'm glad some people do it, but it's not where I'm fully engaged—there are things I care more about, and I want to give them my time. That is true for all of us: there are things we care deeply about and things we care about only to some degree. Being aware of the deeply held cares lets us tap that energy to propel our behaviors. It doesn't matter where or how you opt in: Just opt in somewhere with an accomplice mindset and race-first perspective. Don't feel bad because you can't do all the things. Just do what you can do—and actually do it.

In a recent conversation with a client, Michael, we discussed his goals. As I work on identifying goals, I help individuals or teams hone their lanes. Once we articulate focused lanes, goals are more meaningful and more specific; without lanes, goals can be arbitrary or disconnected from the people who have to achieve them. Michael was very, very clear about his personal lane: "I want to make this organization one hundred percent antiracist." He was new to his organization, and creating an equitable environment there was his entire lane, the focus of all his attention and energy. He was not putting any attention into public school education, healthcare, or any of the myriad other lanes he might have chosen. He defined his lane as this organization and the people within it. Within his first six months using a race-first lens he:

- Increased folks' salaries to right-set people who had not been paid equally.

- Converted the sales team's compensation from a commission pay structure to salaries to create equity among the team members.

- Implemented an open-door policy to engage in transparent conversations with everyone.

- Centered their geographic community in key decisions made inside their organization.

- Used the "What do we know? What do we need to learn?" framework and created content at his organization to teach people what they need to know, not just what they want to see or hear.

In other words, Michael took his role as an accomplice at work to heart, and that is where and how he is burrowing away. He approached his tasks with everything he had because he identified his lane. His energy was completely focused, and he used his attention to make those decisions and changes. He was chipping away at the metaphorical boulder with dedication.

Another client, Tim, was a leader at a financial company but found his lane in the criminal legal system. After some of our sessions, he was watching something about criminal justice and it pissed him off. He became a walking encyclopedia of the criminal justice system and different reforms that have been implemented (both successful and not) throughout the country. He was so passionate about the cause that he started going to protests and writing checks to support groups doing boots-on-the-ground work. You might wonder how this lane, which is unrelated to his work, is a useful example in this book about professional work settings and relationships. Remember when I said that who you are at work starts with who you are outside of work? Tim's dedicated accompliceship in the criminal legal system (*yes, I know how that sounds, but you know what I mean*) informs his perspective on everything else, too. We don't turn off our race-first perspective or antiracist questioning when we walk into work. Tim, like Michael, is developing a practice of becoming aware, pursuing an analysis, and then moving to action.

Focusing your lane or lanes is how you make the most impact because your efforts will be put to use in one space. Your energy will be like a laser beam instead of a disco ball. Without a lane you might dabble here and there—and I've found that dispersed attention can be an accidental off-ramp. You'll find yourself either tired from taking random action or worn out and frustrated by your efforts because you don't have a true area of focus. Not to mention, your lack of clarity may cause harm to the people you seek to serve.

I've observed that your why and your lane—what you're willing to work for—often reveal themselves in the places and spaces that piss you off the most or that you love the most. Hear me out. Some injustices really make us upset. We all see many injustices daily or weekly because we live in a challenging world, but we know the ones that get to us. Maybe they make you extra mad, or they make you cry, or they just move you differently than others. In 2022, I witnessed many of my clients getting pissed off–and fueled by—social issues that were front and center in the news cycle, like critical race theory, book bans, transgender rights, gender-affirming care, reproductive rights, and the effects of overturning Roe v. Wade. These issues became clear catalysts for their action.

Injustice or mistreatment of Black women makes me very mad. I refuse to let individuals in my personal or social orbit get away with writing off Black women because they didn't "comply" or were "in the wrong place." I actively point out the ways that writing Black women off perpetuates treatment that goes back hundreds of years. I will fight tooth and nail and call out every inequitable expectation put upon Black women because they—we—deserve more. And I do all of that because that treatment is deeply offensive to something I'm willing to work for: Black women. To support them, I:

- Coach them
- Offer sponsorship
- Donate money to their causes
- Buy their products
- Seek them out first when I'm looking for services
- Support their political campaigns
- Started The Woke Coach so they don't have to go through what I've been through at unsupportive organizations

I know what Black women have gone through over time. I know how Black women struggl and suffer to be seen and heard by the white patriarchy around them. I love Black women for everything previous generations have gone through and what they passed down to me and my generation. My drive to work for Black women moves me to action every day, even if it's all-caps yelling at people on social media (which, for the record, I don't recommend).

You may move to action because you love something so much you believe everyone should have it and love it as much as you. When you experience something, and you're like, "Oh my God, I just love this. It makes me so happy, and I want everybody to have this opportunity!" you know you've tapped into something you're willing to work for. Maybe that's musical theater—you love the way it taps into creativity and imagination, and that is something you want every person to experience. Or maybe it's basketball because it taught you so many lessons about perseverance and teamwork that you took into adult life. Those keywords, "Everybody should have this opportunity" or "I want everyone to know this" will drive you to action. You'll learn everything about what you can do in that space, talk to other people about it, and probably volunteer so others can access and love that thing too. And, boom, you're moving to action around that thing. That's what accompliceship looks like.

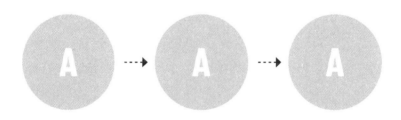

PAUSE FOR AWARENESS AND ANALYSIS

What do you know now that you didn't know before?
What made you engage with this book?

MOVE TO ACTION

Name Your Why

What is *your* why? It has to be something bigger than you, and it has to be something that will keep you connected to this work. It doesn't have to be this long, drawn-out thing. It can be simply, "I want to make this world a better place." That's enough of a why. You don't need a soliloquy, but you have to have a why, and it has to be authentic.

To help define your why, ask:

- What is a life experience or anecdote that underscores why I'm engaging with this book?

- What's my greatest motivation, and what are some things that really matter to me?

- What are my guiding principles? What guides you and what you care about are the direct throughline to your why.

- What vision or outcome could help me take more antiracist actions?

- If there were no barriers to getting it done, what aspect of the world that we live in would I change? Why?

Choose a Lane

Whatever you are interested in—art, education, music, healthcare, voter registration, travel, environmentalism—will have elements of racial inequity. Racism and its effects have touched every single part of our world—including the places that we work. Find that thing that you love reading about, learning about, doing something about, and focus on that with an emphasis on racial equity. Choose a lane at work too. Is it employee retention, diverse hiring, communication, vendor selection, community partnerships, or overall inclusion? I promise that your lane will have a history of racist practices and a current, inequitable circumstance that could use your effort.

To choose a lane, consider:

- How do I spend my spare time?

- What do I enjoy learning about? What do I love sharing with other people?

- What issues do I care about the most?

- What subject matter or industry (maybe aside from your own profession) do I have a connection to? For example, I have a friend whose child was very sick when she was a baby. My friend spent hours, days, and weeks inside hospitals, talking with all the people who worked there and observing what was going on. This experience, while not related to her job, embedded healthcare equity into her lived reality.

- What injustice am I currently furious about?

- What group of people would I most like to support?

You will find that your lane overlaps with other lanes. Our world is full of overlapping and intersecting lanes, each of which feeds into others. You may be doing more good than you think by being intentional. But starting the learning process—the language, the issues, the history—is what choosing your lane is all about.

CHAPTER 8: GET CURIOUS

Nothing Is As It Appears

Hey Siri: "What are cumulus clouds?" "How many feet are in a mile?" "What does it mean to be right-brained?"

Hey Alexa: "What does prix fixe mean?" "Who shot J. R.?" "What is throwing shade?"

If we went to your computer or phone right now and looked up your search history, what would we find? I bet it would be a whole range of topics, from random facts to home improvement how-tos to some takeout options in your neighborhood. We all seek out information about a lot of things throughout our days, out of practicality or necessity, but often out of—you guessed it—curiosity. At that moment, you just want to better understand something you don't currently, or you want to know more about something you know a little bit about.

Accomplices know there is always more to learn about history, people, situations, and moments. There is always more to know, period. About everything.

CURIOSITY IS THE SEED OF OUR LEARNING. WHATEVER WE ARE CURIOUS ABOUT WE WILL TAKE THE TIME TO LEARN MORE ABOUT.

We will research, read, and keep pursuing those topics. What you're willing to work for and curiosity go hand-in-hand in a critical way; once you know what you're working for, a culture of curiosity enables you to fully and wholeheartedly pursue the topics and issues that you care about with a race-first perspective. As we think back to the Three A's—awareness, analysis, and action—curiosity plays a major role in driving this cycle. As the seed of our learning, it drives us to inquire about what we don't know (awareness), and when we learn more, we have more to access as we embark on our learning and understanding journey (analysis). Then, when we know more, we can act in more knowledgeable and appropriate ways (action).

A culture of curiosity for an individual, team, or organization is rooted in asking questions and not taking things at face value. I always say, "Nothing is as it appears." Every sentence, headline, data point, moment, interaction, and conversation has so many aspects that are not apparent unless we intentionally dig into them. For example, an apparently innocent request to take notes could make the Asian woman who was asked really upset. On the surface you might think, "Wow, she seems disproportionately angry at such a small request." But if you ask yourself a few more questions you might start to perceive that moment differently. *What happened to her before that request that primed her for the response? How might biases and assumptions about Asian women and the horrible stereotype that they're docile or submissive play into what happened?*[51] *What else has the individual who made the request asked of her and other colleagues? How might different identities be playing out at this moment?* Or, in another example, say you get survey data from your staff that shows 75 percent of white employees feel supported by their manager, while only 51 percent of your BIPOC employees feel the same. A curious accomplice would drill down into discrepancy. *Who*

---

51 This study explores some of the ways Asian women have experienced discrimination in the workplace, including expectations of submission: "From Exotic to Invisible: Asian American Women's Experiences of Discrimination," July 26, 2018, *American Psychological Association*, accessed July 29, 2022, https://www.apa.org/pubs/highlights/spotlight/issue-119.

are the managers that the BIPOC report to? How might race and racial identity be playing into this scenario? Are the managers exhibiting racial bias? What are the common characteristics of the managers who effectively support their reports? If we break apart BIPOC into specific racial identifications, what do the numbers show us?

There is never an end to a pursuit of inquiry if it's rooted in curiosity. There is no "Okay, that's done!" moment. Likewise, being an accomplice is a lifelong journey—there will always be more to learn. The more you learn, the more you know; the more you know, the more you know what needs to change and how. It's that whole "Once you see injustice, you can't unsee it" factor that keeps us going deeper and recommitting along the way. Building curiosity into your practice can keep you asking the questions we must always be asking.

A culture of curiosity prioritizes inquiry over answers. This does not mean that we don't seek answers. It simply means that exploration and inquiry must be part of the process and motivation if we are to get good answers. A culture of curiosity refuses the status quo for the status quo's sake. Have you ever hung out with a kid in the three-to-five-year-old age range? If so, you know what kids do: ask questions. All. The. Dang. Time. *Why this? Why that? How does that work?* I can remember watching *Family Guy* with my nephew when he was about four years old. Because it's really adult content presented in cartoon form, we each liked it for different reasons. (I know, it's not what I should be watching with him, but I'm the cool auntie!) I would, of course, be cracking up at the adult jokes or talking to the TV, and he would ask questions like, "What are you laughing at? Why is he going to the car? What's so funny about that?" The questions were both frequent and endless. This isn't always fun when you're trying to just get through a book or television show with a kid, but the reality is, we should all approach the world in a more childlike manner. At every turn we should be asking: *What's behind that? How did we get here? Who does this circumstance benefit? Who is left out? What is the history of this concept or idea?* If we do this consistently, we won't take what we "know" for granted. We won't just roll with the status quo simply because it's always been that way.

One of my clients, Jennifer, exhibits such a great spirit of curiosity. If curiosity is the seed of our learning, her seed was planted after the 2016 US presidential election, when the election results revealed that the world she thought existed wasn't real. She was confused; all of a sudden, things didn't seem just and she couldn't put her finger on the what, the why, or the how of it all. Her first steps were entirely personal—she joined the From Ally to Accomplice community outside of work and embraced her antiracist journey as a white woman. As she learned more and more, she started to broaden how she understood the issues. One evening, after a session, she and I had a short but powerful conversation. "As I go through this journey, I keep thinking about how much all these conversions and topics intersect with my work. Because this work was so transformational for me, I can only imagine what this work could do for my organization!"

I couldn't have agreed with her more. She was the executive director at a small nonprofit that connected corporations with volunteer opportunities in the community. When she started her job, the organization was in a bit of a flatlined place. Financially they weren't growing, the staff was all white, and the right roles weren't filled by the right people. She knew she had to make changes, but she wasn't sure what those specific changes were. After joining From Ally to Accomplice, she realized accompliceship could drive not only *what* she changed at the organization, but also *how* it changed. And so we engaged in a program that included our signature components plus some specialized modules. She and her team relentlessly examined themselves and their organization with the bold, guiding question "Are there ways we are unintentionally causing harm in the communities we seek to serve?" We dove into some pretty big issues that were important to their context. We started with the self-awareness piece around Jennifer's racial identity and the racial identities of the people within her organization. Then we got into the history of nonprofits and why they exist in the first place. We explored the dynamics of bringing corporate employees (who we know are disproportionately white) into community organizations (many of which serve communities who are not white) and the kinds of entitlement and white saviorism that may permeate those interactions and relationships. We reviewed the company's policies and procedures, and we carefully dissected the language they used in their mission, vision, and values. Then we facilitated conversations and engagements with some of their corporate partners to extend and expand how deeply they explored their guiding question and to fully understand the implications of partnerships.

"It's funny, Seena," Jennifer said, "but when I started my executive director role, I wrestled with how to be the best leader I could be. I knew I needed to engage with tools and knowledge beyond my existing perspective, but I had no idea what that meant for me within the context of this organization. When I learned about being an accomplice, and especially the idea of using a race-first lens, I realized that was it. It has changed the way I approach my work as a leader, and it has truly transformed how I see everything around me. It's a new lens by which I view the world."

Jennifer allowed her curiosity to lead her in a deeply personal transformation, and she was so open that it led her to take a bold next step to examine everything about the organization. In her own words, "We are able to hold each other accountable and apply an antiracist framework to everything we do. We repeatedly step back and reflect on our language, the way we're showing up, and the role that we play as an organization." She has more BIPOC employees than she's ever had, she has the right people in the right roles, and she is having the right conversations with her corporate and community partners. She is a thought leader on equity and inclusion in the volunteer sector. And it all started with basic questions about herself and her circumstance that she pursued with great energy.

Jennifer's story demonstrates that when we're genuinely curious, and when we are okay with what we learn along the way, even when (maybe especially when) it contradicts or upends something we knew before, we find something deeper and more truthful on the other side. Curious minds want to get to the truth, even if it is challenging. And when we get there, it's not always easy to engage with the truth, but it's necessary.

A culture of curiosity can challenge traditional ideas of leadership. If one of the primary qualities of a fierce accomplice is knowing that you can always know more, then the reverse is also true: you must admit and humbly lean into the fact that you have a lot left to learn. Creating a culture of curiosity requires that you move forward always assuming that you don't know everything you need to know in any given situation. This isn't a natural disposition for a leader, I know. For leaders who have been conditioned to believe they are, or have to be, the smartest ones in the room, this can even feel like an affront. Yet it's a necessary adjustment because, given the high percentage of white-identified people in leadership positions, I can confidently say that no leader knows everything about racialized experience or race and its history.

A culture of curiosity is one in which everyone can and should ask questions. This upends the typical workplace hierarchy in which the person in the leadership role is considered the smartest and the entry-level folk are considered the greenest, the ones with the most to learn. Yet when you value curiosity and different perspectives, there is no hierarchy. No single person is *holistically* more knowledgeable; in a culture of curiosity, the best questions are the best tools, and good questions can emerge from people in any role.

CURIOSITY CAN FIX A LOT

While it's challenging at times, curious questioning is one of white leaders' most direct antidotes to the fear that comes up when talking about race, racism, and all of their implications. When I talk to white clients about their fears, we often find that fear rooted in being afraid of messing up—they don't want to offend or come across as ignorant. In all these emotional situations, a culture of curiosity can help.

When you are genuinely curious, you seek *understanding*, not knowledge. You want to make sense of things, not acquire pure, objective knowledge. When approaching race and racial lived experiences from a perspective of understanding, without expecting a single simple answer, you're already in a more productive mindset. Understanding requires more in-depth work than searching for knowledge. A curious perspective helps you ask better questions, which you'll frame as open-ended rather than limited to yes/no or one-word answers.

Perhaps most importantly, getting curious can help fix one of the most insulting things that BIPOC experience: the willful ignorance of white folks. Willful ignorance is making a bad-faith choice to avoid becoming informed about something so as to avoid having to make the decisions that such information might prompt. Ignorance shows up so many ways: as someone being completely unaware of the concerns and issues facing groups of people unlike themselves, as not understanding or wanting to understand how microaggressions harm folks, and more.

Getting curious about issues confronts the ignorance we're all walking around with every day. Consider the examples above and other situations, such as boards of directors or professional associations. People say they want diversity and then act counter to that goal by pretending they don't know why they are not achieving the diversity that they seek. There is always something that we don't know, and oftentimes we know we're ignoring certain issues. Again, turn to questions like: *What's behind that? How did we get here? Who does this circumstance benefit? Who is left out? What is the history of this concept or idea?* You will learn if you ask, and the more curious you get, the less uninformed and more aware you'll be. Understanding is a natural byproduct of curiosity. The truth is, all of the information you need to know more, learn a different perspective, and go beyond the basics is at your fingertips.

Emotional Labor or Emotional Tax

Curiosity can go completely off the rails when folks ask BIPOC inappropriate questions about their race, their background, or the cultural group to which they belong (or are perceived to belong to). Asking BIPOC to explain personal details or to be stand-ins for an entire group of people is asking them to engage in emotional labor.

Emotional labor is the invisible energy and time that people put into tasks, conversations, or interactions at work that make them labor on behalf of someone else. To be clear: not *in support* of someone else, but *on behalf* of someone else.

The term was first used by sociologist Arlie Russell Hochschild in her 1983 book *The Managed Heart* to describe paid work that involves managing—and sometimes suppressing—your own feelings to fulfill the emotional requirements of a given job. The term was subsequently expanded by journalist Gemma Hartley in her book *Fed Up* to include "the unpaid, often unnoticed labor that goes into keeping those around you comfortable and happy." It's a larger concept, but what is most important for our learning here is how folks from historically excluded groups might experience that at your workplace. Here are a few common emotional labor scenarios in the workplace:

- Asking a BIPOC about their racial identity or racialized experience with the goal of informing yourself.

- Expecting a lone Black or brown person to have an opinion that represents their identity. For example, feeling like you've done due diligence if you had a Black employee read a statement about Black Lives Matter.

- Talking to a colleague about a recent event that could trigger their individual or collective trauma.

- Assuming that someone from a particular identity group will support, assist, or act as a caretaker. For example, expecting a woman to take meeting notes or a Black person to clean up the room after a brainstorm. (This happens. A lot.)

The mistake of requesting emotional labor is what occurs when people are unaware of their biases and assumptions. This is why awareness is the foundation of this book. Biases and assumptions hurt people from historically excluded groups and force them to choose between doing uncompensated, burdensome work or saying no, which might be taken as confrontational or uncooperative. Do your own work, lead your own learning, and remember that no group is a monolith.

PERSONAL VERSUS SITUATIONAL CURIOSITY

Let's call out a giant elephant in the room: Folks can ask some very insulting questions and make some very uninformed choices under the guise of curiosity. Curiosity itself is neutral; it's how you use it that matters. Learning, exploration, and inquiry can be helpful in some circumstances, but they can also cause hurt. For example, it's useful to learn from the world around you and to put yourself into new situations and simply observe. It's harmful to ask an individual probing questions about their identity without first building a relationship with them or to touch someone's body (meaning their person in general) or clothes without permission. That's just being nosy—when a singular person becomes the source or subject of your inquiry, questions are never okay.

The biggest mistake I see people making here is pursuing personal curiosity when they should be pursuing situational curiosity. Personal curiosity is asking an individual about themselves without contextualizing it within the situation. Situational curiosity is an inquiry about the context and circumstances of a given situation. If a detail or fact is irrelevant to the situation, then it will not rise to the level of an inquiry to pursue. Let's use one of the most common microaggressions that I witness: "Where are you from?" There are very few situations in which the answer to that question is relevant. You might want to know for your own personal curiosity, but that is wholly distinct from employing curiosity to understand the moment or situation at hand better.

Before you pursue a line of inquiry, ask these questions to proceed in more productive and meaningful ways:

- Am I asking something personal? If so, is the context for my inquiry clear and relevant to the situation?

- Can I pursue this line of inquiry on my own, without burdening a BIPOC with it?

- What am I really trying to understand by asking this question, and does the phrasing of the question convey my real intention? How else might this question be interpreted?

- Is there any research I should do before asking this question?

- Are there people in my close circle with whom I can explore this topic and hold each other accountable?

- Do I expect the person I am engaging with to speak on behalf of others? Is that a fair and reasonable expectation?

Have you ever thought, "Should I ask this question? Is it appropriate?" I often share this tip with my clients: if you're nervous about asking a question, it's probably because it's at least a little inappropriate. Listen to that inner anxiety and take that question to the internet. While the internet is deeply flawed in many ways, it is also an incredibly useful first step for questions that might be considered ignorant or demanding of emotional labor. Remember that most of our internet search histories will never be viewed, and take advantage of that.

If you don't know how to ask someone something, look it up. If you don't know why hair is such a personal topic for Black women, look it up. If you're unsure why some religions require prayer times, look it up. If you don't know why certain Halloween costumes are offensive, look it up. There is no excuse for not knowing these days because we have so much information available at our fingertips. Putting some work into exploring and inquiring is more important to you as a leader than knowing everything (which you can't—that's impossible).

Curiosity can be very harmful when folks act on impulse, without getting curious about the reason for their actions. Such unchecked curiosity often stems from a place of privilege. For example, I once attended an event with people I mostly did not know after getting new braids put in my hair, and a white woman—a very wealthy and influential white woman—walked right up to me and gently grabbed some of my braids. She stroked them a bit while asking me about the braiding process. I did not know this woman well, and she definitely should have known that touching strangers is always, under any conditions, rude and very uncomfortable. But layer racial dynamics into the interaction and we have this individual, who is used to doing whatever she pleases, trespassing in my personal space and talking about something that is none of her business. She never considered how she would respond if I had run my fingers through her hair in response. This happens to others who fall outside what the dominant culture deems "normal." A close friend of mine is Muslim and wears a hijab, and people she barely knows often walk up and "admire" the fabric by touching it. Another friend of mine who uses a wheelchair tells me that people frequently approach her and move her wheelchair or begin to push her. Most believe they are "helping" her, but they are in fact radically invading her personal space. The fact that these invasions happen over and over again tells us that people don't ask themselves curious questions before engaging with people they see as different. They just act without considering how those actions may impact others. I believe that people sometimes feel like their curiosity can and should be honored ("I can touch her hair," "I can push her chair") no matter the cost to other people in the scenario.

An accomplice will check their curiosity by asking:

- Why am I about to take this action?

- What assumptions am I making about the people involved in this scenario?

- What assumptions am I making about what I have access to?

- What is my intention?

- What possible impact will my actions have on me, the other people, or the interaction?

USE CURIOSITY TO UNDERSTAND YOUR WORKPLACE

Situational curiosity can help you understand many aspects of your workplace. One of the most frequent comments I've heard in my years of engaging with leaders around diversity is "I don't know why we can't find more BIPOC leaders and employees. We have set goals and really made it a priority, yet we're still having a hard time." Now, I happen to know that there are quality candidates in every field who are not white, so I'm always skeptical when companies just can't seem to find them. To help understand their situation, I ask them to take me through a few past hiring processes and describe to me, in detail, how the jobs were advertised, what networks or platforms were used, who reviewed resumes, who was interviewed and who did the interviewing, and what criteria were used to make the final hiring decision. Once we dig into all of this with vigor, we most often learn that they have qualified BIPOC candidates but are consistently choosing white folks over BIPOC. This is an incredibly difficult realization for most leaders to contend with and yet one they could have easily addressed if they had committed to curiosity instead of ignoring the issue.

I often hear from leaders who "don't know" why BIPOC are leaving their organization. They are perplexed and often genuinely concerned, but when we unpack their processes together, we discover they don't do the one thing they should do to get to the bottom of their issues: Talk to the people who are leaving. They don't engage in vulnerable, open conversations about their experiences and why they're leaving. If you want honest answers, sometimes all you have to do is have conversations in which you ask situationally appropriate questions and intentionally listen to the responses. Situationally appropriate questions authentically make space for people's feedback and are scoped to the context at hand: the team dynamics, individual experiences, and individuals' perception of the organization. On some level, leaders know that if they make space for those conversations, they will learn a whole lot about their workplace and culture that they don't really want to know. If these leaders truly pursued a dialogue about why BIPOC employees leave with curiosity, they would learn so much—and maybe even start to produce different outcomes.

Here's what many of the leaders I've worked with are *most* curious about: Are the BIPOC at my company happy? Do they feel like the culture welcomes them? How do they find out? You know what I'm going to say: Ask! Ask very specific, pointed questions about inclusion, belonging, and personal experience with racism in your employee surveys:

- Have you experienced exclusion at work?
- Do you feel like we have a fair and equitable work environment?
- Do you feel a sense of belonging with the company?
- Do you believe we are appropriately addressing DEIAA issues on teams and in the company?
- What are we doing well as it relates to issues of DEIAA? What can we improve on?
- Is there anything else that you would like for us to know?

Leaders often wonder if that will be too much to deal with or feel afraid of what they'll read; some are scared that their wording might be off. Well, I say start somewhere and ask. If you give people the space and place to give honest feedback about their experiences and the culture you're creating, they will tell you.

When you get the responses, move to action with the information. You are not here to play witness; you are here to lead and to make change. The action aspect of this learning is ensuring that the issues they raise are explicitly and directly addressed. If you don't do anything with what you know, your (in)action will speak louder than any antiracist or inclusive proclamations you make.

LACK OF CURIOSITY LIMITS OUR IMPACT

We all need to understand ourselves and others. In business this is especially important because understanding is where empathy and understanding take root. If we don't get curious and ask questions, we will always be coming at situations and interactions from our own limited perspective, and, frankly, our own perspectives are not enough to drive impactful change. Most of us do not have as much awareness about others as we think we do; much of what we think is filtered through our own lived experience. And, as I've said, a white lived experience does not inform white people of what they need to know about the lived experiences of Black and brown people.

Do you spend as much time trying to engage, connect with, and understand the people you work with as you do your target customer? Do you devote as many resources to developing a robust, empathetic culture of understanding inside your organization as you do to marketing and selling outside your organization? The answer is usually no. Organizations spend so much time trying to define and understand the motivations, drives, needs, and contexts of their ideal client or target market from a marketing perspective. Most marketers know this information like the back of their hand, but I'd ask those marketers and their leaders this: What do you know about the people you work with and the histories of different types of people?

Over the last few years, some very public oopsies have shown us just how critical curiosity is to keep businesses out of trouble. Look no further than the 2018 H&M campaign that featured a young Black boy in a sweatshirt that said, "Coolest monkey in the jungle." Or the 2020 Volkswagen ad that showed a miniature world in which a large white hand interrupts the scene and flicks a black man into a restaurant with the name Petit Colon, which translates to little colonist or little settler. In 2020, Prada settled a lawsuit stemming from their 2018 Pradamalia line, which included monkey-like creatures with black faces and over-sized red lips. In 2021, Facebook's artificial intelligence software displayed the prompt "Watch more videos about primates" under a video featuring Black men; the same happened to Google in 2015 when their software classified photos of Black people as gorillas.[52] These companies are far from alone—brands as big as The Gap and Gucci

---

[52] Dustin Jones, "Facebook Apologizes After Its AI Labels Black Men As 'Primates,'" *NPR.com*, September, 4, 2021, https://www.npr.org/2021/09/04/1034368231/facebook-apologizes-ai-labels-black-men-primates-racial-bias.

have committed recent gaffes. These instances confirm that leaders and teams at prominent companies don't know much about people in general, the history of certain people, or even how their products operate in relation to race.

You might wonder how these errors were the result of a lack of curiosity. Several factors likely led to these errors. First, the right people probably weren't in the room. Black folks (plural) should be involved in your creative decision-making process. Period. If you want BIPOC to purchase and use whatever it is you make, get BIPOC into decision-making roles. Second, if BIPOC were involved in these projects, they didn't have permission to speak up and challenge circumstances. Third, if they did speak up, they may have been overruled, as happens all of the time. When BIPOC share their perceptions based on their lived experience, they are often dismissed. This can manifest in comments like, "I think you're being too sensitive" or "Well, that's just your opinion." All three factors are related to curiosity or a lack thereof. Without it, no one will ask serious questions about culture, history, and the BIPOC experience, or about how a product may function differently for people of different races. Without a culture of curiosity, they can write off alternate perspectives or "outlier" use cases. A culture of curiosity requires you to respond to challenges with, "Tell me more about what you're saying" or to investigate product use by a variety of people.

Several people saw the H&M monkey shirt and thought it was cute, yet their inability or unwillingness to ask simple questions about people represented in their ad resulted in terrible PR at the expense of Black people (and Black kids) everywhere. Thanks to social media and the internet in general, we're in a global market now, not just H&M and Pepsi, but also every company large and small. Leaders must remember that the target market is part of a whole, and that whole market consists of people—all people.

If you lack curiosity, you, *personally*, might be limiting your impact not just in the community, but also on your own team. We had a client named Elizabeth who valued "moving fast," a mentality that is very prevalent in the tech industry. She wore it like a badge of honor and approached everything at work with it: people, teams, and processes. When it came to working with The Woke Coach, she had a hard time during the self-reflecting and learning phases because she really wanted to be in the doing phase. She asked to skip parts of our very intentional process, saying, "Let's just get to the work. I'm a bit impatient." She didn't realize that the conversations and reflections were an active part of the work. She believed that moving fast demonstrated to others that she "won't stand for BS" and that "If something's wrong, we fix it immediately."

After working with her for several months, I realized how much this go-fast mentality was limiting what she was able to achieve. First, she was disinterested in any work on self-awareness or curiosity. She didn't want to spend the time pausing, reflecting, and asking questions (which often lead to more questions), so she wasn't prepared and neither were her employees. As a team, they hadn't learned enough or built a foundation that would get them on the same page about the challenges they faced as a company around race. Elizabeth wanted a playbook of what to do and how to do it to address all the issues at her company. Yet answers only come when you're patient enough to take the time to understand yourself, the specific circumstances you and your team find yourselves in, and all that in relation to the outside world. While moving quickly can be a positive strategy, it also gets in the way of deeper understanding because deep understanding never happens quickly. Some things need time to take root, and this is especially true of deeply seeded elements of our work cultures. I can say from experience that curious inquiry isn't a fast process, but it's the only process by which you arrive at meaningful answers.

I also observed how much Elizabeth's behaviors dampened her team's spirits. At the outset they were ready to do the deeper work. But as the CEO, Elizabeth didn't create a culture of curiosity or make space for others to spend time following their lines of inquiry, nor did she want to partner on creative new solutions to the problems the team uncovered through the learning process. As we went through several sessions, I realized that she led her entire company "by the book," and in this book there was only a right way and a wrong way; she lacked the curiosity to consider the organization, the issues, and decision-making from any other perspective. This book—which is really a set of expectations and rules to follow—kept getting in her way. By clinging so tightly to "how things are supposed to be" she missed opportunities to truly evolve—including to more inclusive remote or hybrid work during COVID-19. Instead, early on, she demanded everyone come back to the office, not considering how that would affect individuals or taking the time to explore what people wanted and needed by having conversations with staff. At the start she claimed a commitment to the work, but over time her actions demonstrated otherwise. It slowly infected the entire group's efforts, and eventually I sensed that they lost faith in her ability to lead the work at all.

Doing without learning and curiosity is dangerous. Learning is how we broaden our perspectives; if we're doing without a broadened perspective, we're simply acting from the same set of beliefs, biases and assumptions, and awareness levels as always. There is no way we can be effective accomplices if we haven't changed how we understand the issue or its causes. When Elizabeth wanted to leap into action, I would bring her back to learning by asking, "What do you know now that you didn't know before, and how is that directly informing how you're taking action?" Of course, because she hadn't paused to learn, she often couldn't point to a new or expanded understanding that was informing her behavior. I highly recommend you use this as a barometer for your own journey. Reflecting on what new information you're using to drive your action will help you understand the awareness-to-analysis-to-action trajectory that is so important in this work.

PAUSE FOR AWARENESS AND ANALYSIS

What's resonating with you about what you read in this chapter?

What are you curious about?

Can you get curious about something that makes you feel angry, upset, or enraged? If you care enough to be angry, it's a sign you should learn more and move to action on it.

What might it be like to inspire a culture of curiosity on your team and beyond?

As you consider creating a culture of curiosity, what barriers exist on your team?

What are your organization's DEIAA goals, and what can you get more curious about to support those goals?

MOVE TO ACTION

Question Things . . . All. The. Time.
Something is always happening beneath the surface—there's always more going on that we can see within or outside of our purview.

We know this: how can we figure out what it is? We ask probing questions to expand our understanding of the situation. When we hear about something happening at our organization or in the news, we tend to believe familiar people and sources. I'm asking you to keep questioning. I'm not suggesting that you distrust your usual people or sources, adding other perspectives will help you get beneath the surface. At work this may mean going beyond the colleagues you interact with the most and getting input from new sources.

Being curious is like reverting to that inner child who asks, "Why?" whenever we take in new information.

- Why is this the way it is?
- How else could we do this?
- What else is there to know about the history, current situation, and people involved in this?
- What or who is benefiting? Conversely, what or who is left out?
- Has this always been like this?

Change Your Inputs

An accomplice is always seeking new information, and yet many of us don't seek out suitable sources. We often get news or information from only a few sources, sometimes even just one. And although that single source of input may have good information, it cannot be the only source for learning everything you need to know. Every question that we ask is just a starting point, and no one source will include all the points we should be taking into consideration.

To diversify your inputs, consider:

- Where do you get your information, and how can you diversify your sources?
- What books are you reading? Are there other authors that you should be reading?

- What podcasts are you listening to? What niche podcasts will shine a light on a group or movement that you know nothing about?

- Are there other perspectives that you should be considering? Are you reading original voices talking about their own lived experiences?

- What are three sources you can track to learn new perspectives outside of your typical lens?

- What sources have the most current information on the issues you want to know more about?

- What are the historically underrepresented communities in your city, and what news sources have they created for their communities? Read, listen, or access those.

- How can you create time and space to make expanding your inputs a consistent activity?

Before we continue, I want to pause and reflect on the last two chapters. Being an accomplice starts with us—it's not *about* us, it *starts* with us. That's why finding ourselves and our hearts in the work is so important and effective. When we find our personal pathways, we will increase our personal impact. Knowing your why, choosing a lane, getting curious, and changing your inputs all work together to push you farther and deeper. But it takes all four elements. If you're not using them together, you have a problem. You can choose a lane and not be curious enough to learn the history. You can know your why and still be causing harm. We are all on different journeys, and individual progress is not always sequential or simultaneous, but pursuing and living with all four will make your practice come alive.

CHAPTER 9: ENGAGE WITH DIFFERENCE

We Only Know What We Experience

In chapter one I named a universal truth: BIPOC can't bring their whole selves to work, and white people are afraid of messing up or have no idea how to be truely antiracist (which manifests as fear). I noted that we have to meet in the middle if we're going to create inclusive spaces for everyone. That middle is humanity—when we can see others and ourselves as fully human in all our uniqueness–which is based on our differences. As you hopefully know by now, our lived experiences are very different based on myriad factors, and racial identity creates the biggest differences. If we are to see others as fully human when they do not speak, act, look, sound, or move through the world as we ourselves do, we must engage with difference. It's how we widen our own apertures and begin to experience more than our usual and familiar people, places, and things.

In the United States today, we interact most often with people like us. BIPOC know whiteness because we have to understand it and live in relation to it. But in the sessions I host, many white folks admit to not knowing much about people with a different history and culture. They admit to knowing only Christian holidays and speaking only the English language. Most of their friends and family members are white.

They have had limited exposure to accounts of enslaved people and do not know the intricacies of the Reconstruction era or the Jim Crow era. Because of this, white folks have very little practice in thinking about others' cultures and experiences in relation to their own.

Yet difference is our future. By around 2044, the United States will have a majority-minority population.[53] The non-Hispanic white population shrank by 8.6 percent over the last decade and now accounts for 57.8 percent of the US population, the lowest percentage on record.[54] Between 2017 and 2021, there was a nearly 25 percent increase in the number of people who self-identify as LGBTQIA+.[55] A 2018 article from Pew Research stated, "By 2040, Muslims will replace Jews as the nation's second-largest religious group after Christians. And by 2050, the US Muslim population is projected to reach 8.1 million, or 2.1 percent of the nation's total population—nearly twice the share of today."[56] Right now, up to four generations are working side-by-side in the workforce. Difference will be everywhere before too long—and is already around us if we look for it. So, if we're going to get to that point where we see each other as members of the human race, as so many racism- and xenophobia-deniers wish us to do, or to the point where equality laws actually result in equal treatment, we must ensure that equity exists.

As we think about enacting our practice and leading people inside an organization or being part of a team, it's important to develop literacy and behaviors around difference: recognizing difference, making sense of difference, respecting difference, and championing difference. Difference exists only in relation to the status quo. If

---

[53] Jonathan Vespa, Lauren Medina, and David M. Armstrong, "Demographic Turning Points for the United States: Population Projections for 2020 to 2060," *Census.gov*, issued March 2018, updated February 2020, https://www.census.gov/content/dam/Census/library/publications/2020/demo/p25-1144.pdf.

[54] Joseph Ax, "New U.S. census data shows white population shrank for first time," *Reuters*, August 12, 2021, https://www.reuters.com/world/us/us-release-census-data-used-legislative-redistricting-2021-08-12/.

[55] Jeffrey M. Jones, "LGBT Identification Rises to 5.6% in Latest U.S. Estimate," *Gallup*, February 24, 2021, https://news.gallup.com/poll/329708/lgbt-identification-rises-latest-estimate.aspx.

[56] Besheer Mohamed, "New estimates show U.S. Muslim population continues to grow," *Pew Research Center*, January 3, 2018, https://www.pewresearch.org/fact-tank/2018/01/03/new-estimates-show-u-s-muslim-population-continues-to-grow/.

there were no "normal," there would be no "other." Yet, because the status quo does exist and is upheld with fervor and consistency, we have to continuously make space for difference. To be clear: I'm not claiming that people who don't fit within the status quo are "different"—this isn't a label I'm applying to folks. Black people are Black people, Indigenous people are Indigenous people, trans people are trans people. But the status quo requires continual validation of our differences in order for our humanity to be registered by the dominant culture. When we design for and accommodate difference, we make space for all people to bring their full, unique selves to work.

Differences are the spaces between how individuals move through and understand the world. In engaging with difference, you observe the distance between your current perspective and the new perspective you're learning about, and you ask what those differences may mean for the individuals involved. For example, if you're a cis, white, heterosexual man, you might read about revolutionary trans activist Marsha P. Johnson and recognize how you aren't alike and what that may have meant for her life by asking:

- What are the circumstances and systems that impacted her life, and how would those circumstances and systems have impacted me differently?

- How was she treated by others, and how does that compare to how I am treated by others?

- How were her lived experiences different from mine?

I say difference is humanity because it allows our individual experiences to inform how we interact with and understand each other.

Lived experience is the well we each draw from. This well contains your biases and assumptions. It contains the limits of what you consider normal, appropriate, and acceptable. And it contains what you've learned over your lifetime. The more you have in that well, the more you can offer to and understand about others; the further you can go beyond the superficial generalizations and stereotypes we continue to apply to people who are unlike ourselves. Engaging with difference allows you to humanize people in ways that you might not access with no real sense of their story or who they are. For example, art can be a gateway to understanding others' lived experiences. Attending exhibitions, plays, or watching documentaries created by BIPOC that share views into their lived reality is one way to see the creators, and people who look like them, as more fully human. If you watch the movie *TILL,* you start to understand the strength it requires to be a Black mother in the world, which may chip away at the stereotype of the "angry Black woman." Every new experience with difference deepens your understanding and offers more complex and nuanced details about people who are unlike you. And you can use that new perspective in everyday interactions.

Understanding difference allows you to be more empathetic and to observe things from other perspectives. For example, you might realize, "I don't have any issues around law enforcement, but some people don't have that same luxury." The understanding allows you to reconcile that differences in race mean not every person has the same options that you do—to buy a home in any neighborhood, refinance your home without issues, or be pulled over without incident. Others have a different perspective on and lived experience with those same activities. You start to witness situations where what happens is different for white people than for BIPOC, all because of the systems and structures in place. You begin to be able to hold two truths, or many truths, at once.

BECAUSE LIVED EXPERIENCE INFORMS EVERYTHING ABOUT THE WAY WE MOVE THROUGH THE WORLD, THE BEST WAY TO BE

WELL INFORMED IS TO CHANGE AND BROADEN YOUR LIVED EXPERIENCES.

One of my most important, overarching recommendations to you as a burgeoning accomplice is to go outside your comfort zone to regularly push the boundaries of what you experience and "know" to be true about the world. Every day, ask yourself, "How can I move out of my comfort zone to learn something new or have a different experience?" When you do this, you broaden what you know about others and ultimately about yourself as well.

WHAT ARE THE BASICS OF ENGAGING WITH DIFFERENCE?

On paper, difference may not seem so hard. You may be able to think of a handful of relationships or circumstances in which you feel like differences are present. Perhaps it's racial difference in your workplace or political difference within your family. Are you engaging with the difference or are you trying to downplay or ignore it? Are you seeing it but then trying to connect around anything other than the difference? Borrowing from the definition of cultural competence, the reason to engage with difference is to develop an ability to "understand, appreciate and interact with people from cultures or belief systems different from one's own."[57] Seeking out the differences and then appreciating, not erasing, them is critical because it is how you make room for individual experience.

How do you shift your lived experience?

---

57 Tori DeAngelis, "In Search of Cultural Competence," *Monitor on Psychology* 46, no. 3 (March 2015): 64.

Step 0
Expose yourself to new cultures and folks who have stories that are different from your own. Why is this step numbered zero? Because this is the baseline, the step that doesn't actually count unless you take the subsequent steps.

Step 1
When you find yourself in new environments, reflect on what you're experiencing. Ask yourself:

- What parallels exist between my experiences and the new experiences I'm creating for myself?
- What are the differences?
- What made those differences possible?
- How might those differences still positively or negatively impact people today?

In addition, take time to just be. If you're curious enough to be somewhere new, the people around you will often be glad that you came.

Step 2
Continue to learn the new world you have been exposed to. Attending one event or reading one article isn't engaging with difference; ongoing exposure with new aspects will create the lived experiences you need to inform and expand your perspective.

Extra Credit
Take someone with you! Bring your family or a friend who also wants to expand their perspective. Don't do the learning alone: After whatever it is you're taking in, having a robust conversation will deepen your learning and cement the experience in your mind.

If you're thinking, "Seena, there has to be more to engaging with difference than that," I assure you that this is it. While there is a lot you can do *after* you engage with difference and broaden your perspective, the act of engaging with difference is simple. Now remember, folks, don't go into places and just watch people. Engage! For example, attend an open house at a synagogue or other religious spaces or a festival celebrating a culture other than your own, or watch a TV show created by and featuring Black people (for example, I love *Abbott Elementary*). All of these circumstances are available to you and created for participation.

Without intentionally engaging with difference, most of us will move through our days interacting with people mostly like ourselves and going to the same places we typically go, watching the same kinds of media and eating the same kinds of food, never stretching too far from the usual. If you're always around the same people and environments, you'll have all the same outcomes in the spaces you create for yourself. Expanding can be as simple as examining where you shop, where you worship, what you read and watch, and what you listen to—each is an opportunity to do things differently. The accumulation of daily, weekly, and yearly activities is our lived experience, and each new day, week, year is a chance to expand that experience further.

There are more opportunities than ever to engage with information and cultures beyond what you're used to. Going beyond—widening your aperture—may get you into territory that is new and unfamiliar, and that is exactly the point. Take every chance to expand on what you think you know, and when new information that challenges or alters what you've learned before, keep expanding your understanding. For example, you might believe you have an awareness of Indigenous issues, but when you engage with an Indigenous person from a particular tribal affiliation or region, they might correct something you say. Take that in and adapt. That correction is a gift of new information. No culture is a monolith, so you will never know everything; you are simply adding new water to your well. *Knowing* isn't the point . . . *learning* is.

As much as you may want clear directions, I can't tell you exactly what engaging with difference will look like for you. It's impossible for me to prescribe you some specific actions and experiences to broaden your perspective. Only you can know. But I will recommend exploring political, racial, cultural, religious, gender, age, class, geographic, ability, neurotypicality, and sexual differences to practice making space for difference. Moreover, I suggest striving to expose yourself to the most historically excluded differences first, as they have been most omitted from our most common experiences. That could mean visiting a historical center celebrating Hmong culture rather than going to a Western art museum with the family. It might mean attending a virtual dialogue between members of Indigenous tribes instead of watching your usual evening TV show. Look for your gaps, the topics or situations with which you have the least real lived experiences.

While I can't tell you exactly what to do, I have one warning: Don't start the practice of engaging with difference at work. Start in your personal life (remember, this is self-work!), and then bring your broadened perspective to work. The experiences you create outside of work will give you some practice for being with and making sense of difference, and you can bring that expanded understanding to folks and issues at work.

If you're still worried about making mistakes when you engage, I have a story that may help. I spoke on a panel a few years back, and after a lengthy conversation about race at work, we opened the floor for a Q&A. A young woman stood up, and said, "Seena, this question is for you. I am from a rural community that didn't have a lot of diversity, and I'm at this event because my industry doesn't have a lot of diversity. So, I guess, I'm wondering . . . how do I make Black friends?" I respected the directness of her question (some people will really draw out an uncomfortable question like that), but

I always wonder why some people believe engaging with people who aren't like them is so different from engaging with people who are. I didn't want to say all of that, so I responded, "Well, how do you make white friends?" I was poking a little fun at her—I thought she could take it—but the reality is that you, like this young woman, already have what you need to be a good friend, colleague, and partner to your BIPOC employees. Use the same interpersonal skills you use in every other situation, but with a greater level of sensitivity and awareness of where your lived experiences diverge.

ENGAGING WITH DIFFERENCE AT WORK

Coaching leaders over the years, especially in the last few, I've heard many confide about how difficult their DEIAA results have been to process. Many don't understand why this is. In an introductory meeting with a new client, Jessica, I asked about her organization's DEIAA efforts. Jessica immediately looked uncomfortable, wringing her hands and nervously clearing her throat. She sighed, "It's been a roller coaster, Seena." I asked her to explain the challenges in more detail, and she confessed, "We've really been trying. We set DEIAA work as a strategic priority more than two years ago, we brought in trainers to guide our teams, and Seena, to be honest with you, we haven't made nearly the progress I'd hoped we would. Our BIPOC team members have shared feedback, and we have a long way to go to get where we want to be."

Leaders like Jessica feel frustrated that they can't seem to figure out how to "do" DEIAA. I hear this from new clients time and time again, and when we meet I can immediately see what could be holding them back: their management team or the people around them are all white or majority white. This means they are trying to make decisions about equity and inclusion, but the team doesn't have any BIPOC (or people with another form of difference) who could contribute to growing a culture of inclusion by drawing on their personal knowledge, expertise, and perspective. Even if you've done learning around diversity and inclusion, have gotten curious and changed your inputs, you can't fully embody another perspective. The only way to broaden your perspective at work is by bringing people unlike yourself into the conversations and planning, and then directly and explicitly empowering them to use their lived experience to shape the outcomes.

DEIAA efforts require engagement from nonwhite perspectives because the concepts of diversity, equity, inclusion, and access are all rooted in difference—our most persistent difference (race) must be present in order to create space for any difference at all. A necessary factor in equitable and inclusive environments is making sure that everybody has exactly what they need—and to do that, you must deeply understand what individuals need. You don't have to read minds or guess who needs what just because you're a leader. That's never going to work. Just like couples who have been together for years can't read each other's minds (occasionally you might get it right, but there are always surprises, right?), you will never be able to "just know" what individuals need in and from your workplace.

The most efficient and effective way to create equity and allow for differences is to make space for people to articulate their needs. This may be in employee surveys or some other official, widely accessible feedback mechanism. You can have a genuine open-door policy that allows people to come to you with their own agendas. You can ask specific questions in meetings that encourage individuals to share their thoughts and feelings, such as "How am I finding you today? How can I support you? What other support might you need? Are there things you need that you do not have?" Open questions give folks the opportunity to tell you what's on their minds and what could help them at that moment. "How am I finding you today?" is a particular favorite of mine and one I use all the time in my work. It gives leaders an opportunity to engage with people wherever they find themselves in that moment. It allows for nontraditional responses and sharing the truth of folks' current circumstances. These questions generate dialogue because they require more than just yes-or-no responses and demonstrate genuine care about others' circumstances.

Then, in the expressive conversations that such questions elicit, allow for the fullest, most robust responses possible. Get curious and encourage dialogue until you really understand the needs expressed. Ask follow-up questions and clarify points you don't understand or that will help you see their points of view more fully. And then, as always, move to action. Solve for what you can; don't let their sharing go unacknowledged and their needs go entirely unmet.

Culture is the sum of our lived experience, and each person will come to spaces with a variety of lived expereiences and expectations. As you develop a practice around asking and learning about individual needs, the personal details, stories, and ideas you learn will help you deepen your empathy well. You will start to understand issues that impact your team members based on their personal or racialized experiences, see differences, and design and solve for those differences.

WHAT IS THE OPPOSITE OF DIFFERENCE?

"We're all part of the human race."
"All lives matter."
"Can't we all just get along?"
"We're more alike than we are different."
"I just don't see color."
"You're being divisive by bringing up race."

Have you ever said or thought of any of the statements above? Some of these may come from a well-intended perspective, but they are the opposite of difference; they minimize very real and drastic differences among people. A minimization mindset, as it's called in DEIAA work, emphasizes commonalities over differences. At first glance, this approach may appear positive: Finding common ground can be an effective way to build a relationship and understanding. Yet there are dangers in minimizing. It de-emphasizes the differences. I've underscored throughout this book and creates a set of expectations, explicit or implicit, that others are supposed to be the way we ourselves are—and that's never true.

Minimizing happens to me all the time, but one conversation in particular stands out. A friend who was newly appointed to an editorial role at a magazine asked if they could publish an interview with me about "this moment" in the aftermath of George Floyd's murder. People were asking, "What can we do?" and my friend wanted to respond to the surging interest. I agreed, and shortly thereafter a white writer—let's call him Paul—reached out to me and scheduled a call. I didn't have a lot of background information on him (I usually do my homework) but figured we would find our way through the conversation. When I got on the call, Paul opened almost immediately with "I understand what you're going through as a Black woman in the world right now, after George Floyd died. I was bullied as a kid because I was gay, and the pain and fear are still with me." He went on, but I had stopped listening because I was so taken aback. "You know," I said when he finished his introduction and personal story, "there is an inherent difference between me being Black and you being gay and what that means in a US context, which is a racialized society." He paused, a little surprised, but then doubled down on how sad he felt after being bullied, I guess assuming that it was similar to the sadness and pain I felt at that moment. I let him talk; I knew my experience was different, and if he couldn't understand that, I wasn't sure I needed to convince him of it. Then he said, "Okay, let me ask you a question: What is it like when people describe you as an angry Black woman?" Whaaaat? That was a record-scratching comment. And the end of my rope.

I was filled with sadness at the state of the world. I was doing a favor for a friend, and this is where I found myself. I couldn't hold it in, so I said: "We're going to stop this interview. I have to be honest with you: I don't think you know enough to conduct this interview. I think you need a better understanding of the world we live in to have a conversation about this moment in time. Go do some learning around race, especially your race, and then come back to me." Now, I'm sure he was trying to create rapport with me. I know he believed we had common ground based on "similar" experiences. In reality, our experiences were not remotely the same, and when I raised that point, he did not make space for me and continued to insist on the similarities. He didn't know that what he was doing was damaging: he minimized my lived experience and then fell back on stereotypes of "angry Black women" to try and get to know me as a person. In fact, he assumed that I *was* that stereotype by even asking the question. I should have guessed when the article was explained to me as "tips on how each of us can be more mindfully woke each day in order to better cocreate and respect each other" that I was dealing with someone who didn't fully understand being "woke," as if we can wrap up seeing each other's humanity into tips. In case you're wondering, I never heard from him again, but I did see him comment on a post my company's social media about how much he learned from us.

Minimization is one big microaggression toward people who are considered different from the dominant culture. It's a constant, cumulative reminder that who we are is at odds with who people expect us or want us to be based on their limited experience.

When a minimization mindset is present, we create places and spaces that are not welcoming to people who are different from the status quo. If a place only welcomes the aspects of me that are like other people, there is going to be a lot that I, and people like me, can't bring to the space. If we bring our full selves, we will be bringing differences into white spaces. The CROWN Act exists because my natural hair has historically been deemed "unprofessional."[58] If you really think about it, how can the way my hair grows out of my head possibly be unprofessional? It's literally how I was born! It's not fluorescent green (which is also not inherently unprofessional, but it is a deliberate style choice). Yet Black, or textured, hair is not acceptable because a minimization mindset leads white people to want my hair to look like white hair. Similarity to their hair makes it more comfortable to engage with and sit in meetings with me and my textured hair. A constant desire for sameness, and a discomfort with difference, is the only reason to culturally force Black women to do their hair like white women. As I think back on years of professional experience, it's alarming how much time and money I have spent changing the way I naturally am to fit into spaces that have been designed for whiteness. It's the hair, and also how I speak, my word choices, and my clothing. Over the years I have adapted my preferred ways of expressing myself in order to blend with a set of expectations that aren't natural to me. And I did all this because I received the message that how I am naturally isn't appropriate, and if I want to succeed, or at least survive, I will have to do something to change myself. It's so ingrained that even now, as the president of a contemporary arts institution's board of trustees, every time I get dressed for an event, I debate the size of my earrings, whether I should get rid of my braids, and if my leather pants will be too much. And this is the arts, for crying out loud!

One of the most damaging consequences of minimization is that our day-to-day conversations and interactions aren't honest or empathetic. An acquaintance, Caroline, a white woman recently shared in conversation with me that she had a wonderful relationship with a Black person at work. She felt this relationship cemented her opinion that her workplace was safe for the BIPOC who worked there. She even referred to her Black colleague as her friend. "That's great," I responded. "I'm glad that connection is a good one and that

---

[58] https://www.thecrownact.com/

you two have formed a friendship. Can I ask you a question?" She looked nervous, but politely replied yes.

"What does she do in her spare time? What' your friend's favorite beverage (alcoholic or non-alcoholic)? Does she come from a large family or a small one?"

Caroline didn't know the answer to any of these questions. "Seena, that's not fair," she replied. "Valerie and I talk about our kids from time to time, our favorite comedies, and occasionally we've even had lunch and happy hour. We have each other's backs."

I could see I was getting under Caroline's skin. She truly felt close to her friend Valerie, and here I was challenging her. "Listen, I don't doubt that you and Valerie are friendly and that you both have come to appreciate your working relationship. But my guess is that beyond superficial commonalities, you two haven't gone deep about Valerie's experience as a Black person, right? Have you asked her pointedly about where she feels her race is a liability or a barrier in her role?" She looked away, opened her mouth to say something, then closed it again. She didn't want to admit that she'd never ask her "friend" that, but it was also sinking in that maybe she wasn't allowing Valerie to be her full self.

Going beyond the superficial similarities is essential because it's how we build honest relationships. The strongest relationships are built at the intersection of commonalities and then curiosity. Commonality is how you come together initially—maybe you're on the same team at work, have children in the same schools, or both love rom-coms. But after coming together, curiosity is how you build genuine connection. Curiosity is how you share more of yourself and in doing so allow others to share more of themselves. It's where perspectives, and not just interests, are shared. Real relationships are another way to fill your empathy tank. If you don't have relationships beyond the chit-chat, then your Black colleagues have likely never talked to you in earnest about what it's like to be Black in this country, about the fears we have for our children, or our experiences with law enforcement. If you rarely (if ever) hear a Black perspective and you don't have the lived experience, then when a Black colleague does talk about their reality, you may feel like they're exaggerating (at best) or lying (at worst). Whatever personal experience they have may feel so unfamiliar that you can't place it within your worldview or truly empathize with them.

When we minimize differences, we also minimize other people's humanity. A minimizing mindset or exchange communicates to the person whose differences are being flattened, "The way you are experiencing the world isn't as important to me as the way I experience the world." We are also saying, implicitly, "I don't believe you" or "I don't care." As leaders, our goal is to find ways to connect everyone's humanity. So if someone suggests that some language is ableist, you can create circumstances in which employees talk about their different opinions about language. Then, maybe, the group can come to a consensus and understanding around the different perspectives—some may immediately understand why the team should not use "Hey guys" and others may need more time. But by encouraging dialogue, perhaps you can change some hearts and minds, and even better, folks get some practice in having conversations about difference. But if you dismiss the topic instead of creating space for a conversation about the ableist terminology, you may inadvertently squelch part of who people are—the folks offended or hurt by the ableist language—and what they are trying to bring to your company and culture.

I think hesitant people assume that to make space for others, their own space must be diminished. But that's not true. Humanity is humanity, and if we are building spaces and places that allow for our full humanity, no one is left out. Sure, you might have to behave a little differently or learn a new way of working, but there will always be room for folks who want to build shared humanity.

MINIMIZATION AT WORK

Aside from all of the ways we may individually minimize others, minimization can also be organizational. This is when the systems and practices within a company don't allow for or make space for difference. Some examples include:

Color-Blind Policies

"Color-blind" policies assume that fair or equitable circumstances already exist (though they likely don't). I find that most policies in workplaces qualify as color-blind because they don't center race. For example, assigning only certain holidays as company holidays is color-blind. Juneteenth is a significant day for African Americans but was only recently made a holiday at the federal level; likewise, Martin Luther King Jr. Day has been a federal holiday for years but it isn't recognized equally at the state and local levels. Another color-blind policy is requiring folks to use PTO to recover from racist murders or violence in the news. Such seemingly neutral policies don't affect all people in the same way.

Culture Fits

Hiring candidates who are "culture fits" or with whom the hiring committee would want to "have a beer or hang out" results in new hires who are like the people already at the organization. We can't allow familiarity to win over difference.

Diminishing People's Feedback

Responding with "That would never happen here!" or "That can't be true." or "Are you serious?" upon hearing feedback from BIPOC about their experiences is gaslighting. By leading with disbelief or asking people to "prove" something, you're reducing their experiences.

Reducing People to Their Similarities

This is grouping like with like. For example, asking BIPOC if they know the one or two other BIPOC at the organization or assuming that BIPOC will have the same experiences, concerns, or opinions—remember, no group is a monolith. Also, at a bare minimum, know that you are talking to Michelle and don't call her Camille—the other Black woman in the office.

Disbelieving the Power of Difference

Not understanding how diversity is an asset will inevitably result in any efforts toward diversity being performative at best or stagnant at worse.

After sitting with executives and coaching leaders through difficult race-based challenges, I can tell you that a majority of white leaders just don't know how to be around difference. Or, I should say, they don't know how to center the experiences of others when they seek to engage with difference. To understand this, let's revisit one of the truths about where we now know: The barometer of comfort in this country is set to white. Because this is the case, all things orbit around and are understood in relation to white experiences. Difference, on the other hand, has no central gravitational pull. It's dispersed and distributed among many people and experiences. Because white-identified leaders within a US cultural context have never experienced things that way, they may aggressively (consciously or subconsciously) resist the shift away from white-centeredness.

We know that the places and spaces that will be most successful in becoming inclusive will let the culture ebb and flow with the people. People determine the culture, not leadership. Many leaders are too afraid to allow their workplaces and work cultures to grow and evolve organically because it's hard to let go of the perception of control. Yet I'm here to tell you: allowing for differences will always be an organic, ongoing process (much like being an accomplice) because newness will be ever-present. New differences and new perspectives will come with each new hire and as existing employees learn and expand their understandings.

Often, we minimize because what we know is easier than what we don't know, and it's easier not to know. Minimizing keeps people safe from feeling guilty and shameful. If we don't think of something as hard, harmful, or, in some cases, real, then we don't have to address it. Not only that, but by minimizing it individuals evoke power—saying "I don't see that" effectively invalidates the claim. In fact, minimization in psychology is tied to behaviors of manipulation and abuse. The minimization mind game is a cousin to gaslighting: Both are techniques that downplay lived experiences.

Don't Gaslight

I'm going to be straightforward here: BIPOC can spot expressions of racism, microaggressions, and biases within seconds. We're so tuned into how they unfold that we've developed a very evolved Spidey Sense. One of the most frustrating social phenomena we deal with is people telling us that racist incidents aren't really happening. That's gaslighting, and it can seep explicitly or implicitly into conversations at work.

Gaslighting is when one person undermines another's lived experience by questioning their reality, their perceptions, or their feelings. This can sound like, "Are you sure?" "I think you might be overreacting," or "I don't think it happened like that." It can be questioning whether our experiences happened the way we say they did: "That's not racism, he's just kind of cold." Mmmmhmmm, cold toward Black people. Subtler gaslighting might look like asking BIPOC to "prove" or give evidence of something we said happened or asking if there is any way we might have misinterpreted things.

Differences mean different realities, and this increases the risk of gaslighting. Think back to the leader who said that she never saw racism at her workplace. If she had said that to any of the employees who had shared their experiences with her, she would be gaslighting them. It's not easy or fun for BIPOC to bring up instances of racism. We would much rather come to work and not have to deal with it; if we're bringing it up, it's because we can't ignore it anymore—and no one should want us to.

An accomplice will recognize and fight the inner urge to move toward comfort. You will seek out opportunities to understand, point out, learn about, and take action on the differences that exist in our world. You will grow to be okay with as many versions of normal as there are people around us. You will work to know yourself and your impact on others so well that you can sit in the discomfort that comes when someone else says, "That's your version of things. Here is mine." And you can engage with their reality without defensiveness, guilt, shame, or overwhelm.

When we engage with and make spaces for difference in our workplaces, we gain so much: perspective, new ways of doing things, rebukes to the status quo, growth, development, greater understanding, deeper connections between colleagues, reduction of the fear of messing up, lower turnover, and better recruitment and retention practices. And, ultimately, you cause less harm. As a leader, continually broadening your perspective and modeling that for your team and company is an important part of the work. The notion of expanding and changing and growing, rather than stagnating, lays the foundation for an inclusive environment and an equitable culture. The culture and your environment will always change and grow as you add new people and allow each and every one to bring their full selves.

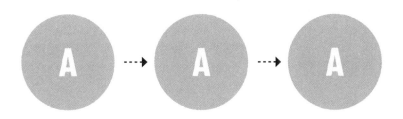

PAUSE FOR AWARENESS AND ANALYSIS

- What's resonating about what you read in the chapter?
- Are there places and spaces where you allow your employees to give you the unfiltered truth about their experiences, especially if they are BIPOC?
- Do you have a tendency toward a minimization mindset?
- How has minimization played a role in your leadership or your worldview?
- How do you respond to difference when you encounter it? Do you acknowledge it, or does it make you uncomfortable?
- How are you developing deeper relationships with people who are different from you so that you can understand how differences show up in your business and how difference plays into the work experience of your employees?

- Where can you take your family or yourself to have different experiences and different engagements (beyond going to a restaurant and getting different food, which is the bare minimum)? What are you reading? What events are you attending?

- To what organizations do you contribute your money and your time? What boards are you serving on? How can you learn about new issues through your philanthropic activity?

MOVE TO ACTION

Look at Data

Difference is not just about engaging with people. It's also about engaging with the different experiences and inequities present in your company and going further to understand how those differences affect the workforce around you. For leaders and managers, data is a helpful starting place that can show you that difference and inequity exist and point to where it is occurring. Productive questions to ask as a leader are:

- What does the data say about where the inequity exists in your industry? Because it's there.

- What do you know about pipeline issues at your company?

- What do you know about your retention rates of BIPOC employees compared to white employees?

- Do you do exit interviews? What do they tell you?

- When BIPOC folks decline your offer of employment, do you ask them why they didn't accept?

Use that data to go deeper. Engage means "to participate and become involved in." So, participate in improving what the data is telling you.

Get to the bottom of what the differences are and why. You can't stop at knowing and say, "Well, that is interesting. Now back to doing things as we've always done them."

Stay Up to Date on Legislation
This book includes many examples of harmful legislation, and in writing it I had to update the list several times. Nearly every state has introduced or passed more bills than I can even track on trans rights, Access to reproductive healthcare, critical race theory, marriage equality, and voting access. Many of these issues we thought of as settled, but people are working day and night to maintain the status quo or even reverse its course.

Know that such legislation, and the public commentary and conversations around them, hurt some of your employees, even if proposed laws aren't passed. As an active accomplice, you must maintain an awareness of legislation unfolding in your area and address the damage it may cause. Had Coca-Cola and Delta gotten ahead of the voting restrictions passed in Georgia in 2021, that legislation may have never passed. Consider:

- What was illegal and legal in the past, and what impact might it still have on cultural or social outcomes?

- What legislation is in motion, and who will be most impacted by it?

- What is your perspective on current controversial legislation? Don't wait until laws are enacted to develop a point of view.

- How are you going to share your perspective and help your employees feel supported and included?

This might feel like something out of your scope of work, but if you can make things better for your employees, that's your responsibility.

CHAPTER 10: START TAKING RISKS

You Can't Just Know a Thing; You Have to Do a Thing

An accomplice is deeply committed to antiracism and is always risking something to change our circumstances. Through this combination—and all the work outlined in this book—you begin to make an impact as a fierce accomplice and move toward being your best, most empathetic self.

Before we continue, let's take another look at the definition of *accomplice* so we can re-root ourselves in why we're taking risks.

> Accompliceship is a proactive practice of ongoing learning and continuous action in relation to what one learns. It is not an identity; it's intentional behavior derived from awareness and understanding and informed by those you seek to serve. Accomplices feel a personal responsibility to rectify the historical effects and current realities of historically underrepresented people's oppression. They take action, educate themselves, and risk their power and privilege for the benefit of others to create a more equitable and just society.

You've seen aspects of this definition pop up throughout the chapters. We've covered how essential awareness and understanding are to this work. We've covered the idea of continual learning and then doing something new based on what you learn. We know what we know, so (again) what are we going to do about it?

We're going to get risky.

This whole journey has helped you prepare for taking risks to make change around you. As a leader, you should be ready to observe when inequities play out and to make calculated and strategic adjustments to your behaviors to produce different outcomes at work. You're prepared to support BIPOC as much as white employees have traditionally been supported and championed. You're also ready to address any pushback you experience as you slowly shift the organizational culture at work. You're preparing cases for why equity and inclusion are important; you're preparing evidence that the status quo isn't equally beneficial to all people; and you're assembling a cohort of like-minded people who will join in the work you're doing. Most importantly, when you commit to taking risks, you hold yourself to a standard higher than just doing something.

When fear is present, we often believe there is risk. But that isn't always the case. You likely don't fear getting into your car or crossing the street in the way you fear calling out an inequity in your workplace. Yet, you have a much higher chance of being hurt while physically moving through space than while addressing inequities. The difference is that you are accustomed to managing the risk of driving or walking. You've done it over and over again, and you've calculated the benefits and risks, so your fear-based emotions have subsided. The same can and will be true of the risks I'm asking you to take as an accomplice: as you participate more and more, your fear will subside. The risks become easier to calculate and tolerate. I've found that for most folks, trepidation, discomfort, guilt, shame, and unfamiliarity get in the way of doing the right thing at times. Taking risks is a direct way to overcome those emotional responses and to become the best, most empathetic version of yourself you can be through continuous action.

The fact is, for white folks doing the right thing doesn't involve that much risk. Comfort or agreeableness are on the line, not your job, life, or health. People just aren't used to moving to action around what we're witnessing or what we learn. So, while I acknowledge that the behaviors in this chapter will feel difficult and put you in unfamiliar circumstances, you will survive. And that's empowering—what you consider risky changes as you grow more confident and more comfortable with the act of taking risks. As an accomplice, you will move to the edge of your comfort zone and continually push the boundaries of what is risky in order to do what's right. Now that's fierce.

So, let's get into some ways you can practice risky behaviors. These aren't all the risks you can or will take, but they are common and accessible actions you can take now to practice antiracism. They are some of the most basic and useful steps accomplices can take to start taking risks.

PREPARE FOR DIFFICULT CONVERSATIONS

I've already mentioned emotional labor and, specifically, not relying on the emotional labor of BIPOC to educate white people about racism, racial identity, or lived experience. As an accomplice, one of the most significant things you can do is prepare for and engage in difficult conversations around racism so BIPOC don't have to carry the entire load. What are these conversations that you should prepare for?

Naming offensive comments, language, or behaviors. Now, I'm not a fan of cancel culture or callout culture—I'm a fan of call-in culture—but you can bring your own style to things. But in this conversation, accomplices name offensive language. Offensive language may be explicitly racist, sexist, ableist, or biased against someone's religion, sexuality, attire, or anything else about a person's identity. Offensive language may have roots in terrible history, even if our current understanding doesn't feel rooted in that same meaning. The bottom line is that offensive language is exclusive, not inclusive.

Some offensive language is so common that it is unnoticed—like using the word *guys* to address a mixed-gender group (assuming a particular type of body) or calling a team meeting a *powwow* (a word appropriated from Indigenous culture and then stripped of its original meaning). Just because word use is common doesn't mean it's not offensive to some people. And if it's offensive to some people, why use it? If simply uttering it excludes a section of society, why keep saying it? It might take learning some new habits, but that's not very hard in the grand scheme of things.

We may come across offensive language with our relatives, neighbors, people in our religious communities, and acquaintances in our social media networks or volunteer organizations. These spaces, where identities, norms, values, and levels of understanding mix, are ripe for witnessing one-off incidents or patterns of behavior that do not align with accompliceship or inclusion. When we call out what we witness, we are not only living the values we've committed to but also signaling to others that racism doesn't have a place in our social interactions. I've heard that in white spaces, white people often assume that other people won't be offended by racially charged statements, or maybe they think other white people will agree. If you do not say otherwise, you confirm this assumption and keep recycling the harm. Read that again. Familiarize yourself with words or phrases that may be considered offensive, even if you're not personally offended. Practice kind corrections. Get comfortable highlighting why these words or phrases should be omitted from use.

In a work context, naming racist or biased comments creates an expectation and an environment in which naming things is expected and okay. If we can name things, learn from the naming, adjust as necessary, and move on, we can create environments that allow for growth. For example, if you're discussing a potential new hire and your colleague assumes gender identity by saying, "he," you can respond with, "Let's not assume it's a man who will fill the position. Let's use 'they' until we know more about the person who accepts the job." Then, move on. You don't have to say, "That's biased"; you can point out a different way and then keep going. If it's an egregious comment, it will warrant more care, but remember that you don't have to justify expecting people to use humane and respectful language.

Pay attention to the words coming out of your mouth too. While "having difficult conversations" suggests communication with others, it's also coming to terms with practices of your own that may need to change. Ask yourself, "Why do I use the word *crazy* in conversation? Are there alternatives that could communicate the same thing without using ableist language?" You don't need to have all the answers; you have to ask better questions of others and yourself. An accomplice asks all the questions and tries to be the best version of themselves all the time.

Basically, shut down all of the racist, ableist shit. It's as simple as that. If clients, constituents, vendors, guests, or literally anyone says offensive things, shut it down. If you're afraid, do it anyway. If you think you're the only one who noticed the racist thing, you aren't. There are people who will back you up but who are also afraid. Be the one to say something.

Conversations with confrontational colleagues as your company is doing DEIAA work. These are the flies in the ointment: those who try to derail things as everyone else is just trying to do good work. In these conversations, knowing the benefits of inclusive environments can help. The data is there to back up any efforts.

That makes me think of a time I was working with a team on inclusive language. I had worked with this group for a few months, so they had started to believe that they were pretty good accomplices. (This always happens—a few months in, people start thinking, "I got this!" and then something new comes up to remind them that this is a continuous journey and you will always be learning new things that throw you off. But I digress . . .). When we got to this lesson, they struggled. One team member in particular was hung up on the word *guys*. He just couldn't get his head around the fact that it wasn't inclusive: "But I say this all the time!" And he was just floored at the thought of changing a word that he uses thirty times a day. He pushed back and asked, "So when can I use it?!" I asked him, "Why do you even have to?" And that often is how you can address cranky colleagues, with the simple question, "Why *not* do this work? Why not make our workplace feel more inclusive?"

Another strategy is to get curious about their perspective rather than try to fight it. If someone is resisting change, ask clarifying questions like: "Did you just say [*egregious comment*]? Help me understand your perspective." or "I'd love to understand how you came to that conclusion, can you talk me through your thinking?" These aren't trick questions—by asking them curious, clarifying questions, you give them space to work through their thought process, and get them thinking more about their behavior by modeling a path toward self-awareness.

Name injustice when you witness it. Whenever we see injustice, inequity, or unfairness, it is our responsibility to say something. We may have been taught to keep our eyes and ears to ourselves, but if we all did that, we'd never make change. It takes collective action to change things. So, if you're at the grocery store or the gas station and you witness someone saying something foul to someone else, step in with as much care and strategy as you can. Don't put yourself or others in danger, but stand up for someone who is being mistreated. The truth is, I could list a whole page of moments when I myself have witnessed unfairness, but I believe we know injustice when we witness it. We know when someone's being given a harder time; we just typically don't address it because we're nervous. Then, later, we might think back to it and wish we'd said something. Don't wish, do it.

Name when someone is focusing on interpersonal or individual racism at the expense of institutional or structural racism. Interpersonal racism is a scapegoat for broader conversations around race and the history of race in this country. It's a way for people to say, "I'm not racist, so we don't need to talk about racism." If you've learned anything so far, I hope it's that, yes, we need to talk about racism and, no, interpersonal racism isn't the only kind of racism. Consciously or not, by limiting conversations of race to individuals, people are gaslighting us. If a white person says that you don't appear to have a race problem at work, I would ask two questions: How do you know? Have you examined policies and practices and not just individual behavior?

Manage up in your DEIAA conversations. Unless we're CEOs (and most of us aren't), managing up is always a part of our jobs. And when it comes to DEIAA at work, we might have to do so because leadership can be fearful of the work. They may want to do the right thing but feel terrified of change, the unknown, messing up, embarrassing themselves, doing it wrong, or being seen as ignorant. But they also have the pressures of being the leaders with a capital L. I'm not excusing it, but I certainly witness leadership teams buying programs and education for staff, drafting statements about inclusion, and empowering committees to do antiracism work, and then, when it comes to personally opting in, stepping back. But if they don't opt in to this work with a greater level of understanding and commitment, the outcomes won't stick. All leaders and managers have to be on board if staff are going to be on board; any hesitation will let others think they can also dip only their pinky toe in the antiracist pool, when we need a total lap-swimming commitment in the same waters as us.

Name others' privilege as well as your own. As you might remember from chapter 4, it's hard to notice privilege. It's often invisible to us until we seek a greater understanding of how we move through the world. Accomplices are bound to encounter folks who don't want to acknowledge their privilege, ever; they get mad when you say that they have it and madder when you say that because they have it, someone else doesn't. Yet, until we are aware of the privilege we have and how it affects our circumstances, we won't see the reality of those situations clearly. So, as accomplices, we have to be willing to shed light on some very basic but challenging aspects of power and privilege. It's like that story I shared about a leader who received feedback that BIPOC at her company experienced racism and replied, "But I don't see anything racist happening." This was a moment to shed light on her privilege and help her realize that she wouldn't be able to see racism because her white privilege keeps it from happening to her.

These are all risky conversations because you're putting yourself out there to challenge someone directly, and often challenging how they experience the world. Even when you do it in the kindest way possible, defensiveness is still a potential reaction. But if you're really committed to bringing an antiracist practice to your actions, speaking up needs to be a huge part of your work. In any difficult conversation, your lived experience and learned knowledge will be your biggest assets. If you experience more and know more, the level of difficulty will diminish, as will your fear. If you're white, you will come to find that whatever risk you take and whatever happens to you as a result of that risk is not nearly as bad as what happens to BIPOC every day in this country. It will be uncomfortable. Your heart might race a bit when you start the conversation, but you will get better and more habitual with your words and capabilities the more you do it.

HIRE BIPOC

Commit to hiring BIPOC. Period. Especially at leadership and managerial levels. Give BIPOC an opportunity to execute on their ideas from a position of power. Ensure they can make as many significant decisions and have as much access to resources as the others on the team (read: white folks). Why? Because if they don't have power, then they're just a token—they won't be able to take action on what they offer as a leader. To make real, lasting organizational change, people need access to power and resources. You cannot make progress on DEIAA without having BIPOC at the power table, listening to and trying their ideas, and seeing what happens when you make absolute equitable decisions. An all-white team can't do DEIAA work without input, guidance, and leadership from BIPOC. Period. No matter how informed and well-intentioned they might be.

Maybe resource allocation is risky. But I'm going to turn it up another notch. If you're engaging as an accomplice, you'll strive to have not just one or two BIPOC on your leadership team. You will hire three. One person stands alone. When there's two BIPOC, white folks can pit them against each other. When you have three, the BIPOC teammates have a critical mass—and that's when they can really start to change things. That may feel difficult because most companies don't have the systems and structures to find, hire, and retain BIPOC at that level and scale. But if you're serious about this work, this is the minimum—the absolute bare minimum.

Let me be clear: I know hiring BIPOC won't immediately create inclusion, but bringing in diverse representation, new perspectives, and potentially new ways of working will expand—and hopefully challenge—your current status quo. When I was a kid, all of my teachers from second through eighth grade were Black people.[59] That

---

[59] A deep honor and reverence for Mrs. Geneva Finney, Mr. Steve Martin, Mrs. Cynthia White, Mrs. Shirley Autry, Ms. Shirley Brown, Mr. Len Amaker, and Mrs. Janie Burgess, to name a few.

meant a lot for my experience as a young Black girl. I saw myself in them, and that allowed me to be my complete self at school and feel like the people around me saw me fully. It meant that while we watched the television series *Roots* for our history lesson, we could talk openly about how it affected us as Black people. We could display our emotions without judgment or fear. It also meant that I had early role models who showed me what I could do and what I could achieve simply by being themselves in their job. Representation matters: People need to see themselves reflected in their circumstances. It allows them the ability to be their full selves.

PROMOTE, PUSH, AND ADVOCATE FOR BIPOC

Once you hire BIPOC, ensure the doors don't get shut in their faces. White leaders have enormous power and privilege. No matter how limited you think you are in your scope of influence, I assure you it's much wider than you think. And you are in a perfect position to give opportunities to people of all backgrounds.

You can identify exactly what experience a BIPOC colleague may need to move up and then take it upon yourself to create that experience. One of my dear friends in the publishing industry had a boss early in her career who demonstrated what it means to advocate for a Black peer. When I asked her what made him such a unique boss, she listed off a set of things that truly made a difference in the trajectory of her career: "He nominated me for a monetary-backed award highlighting my good work, he designated money from the budget to pay for the masters in publishing degree that he insisted I do and even gave me a list of the schools that I should apply to, he sponsored me early in my career as I made embarrassing rookie mistakes—even taking the blame and spending extra time to coach me through how I could do something better. All of this without batting an eye." And now she is a very successful publisher. Could she have gotten there without his advocacy? Of course! But damn, that kind of support is amazing and should be equitably offered at every company.

One thing I hear from BIPOC a lot is that they're passed over for promotions or advancements, and their path toward success is rarely clear. In a recent cohort session, I had a side conversation with a Black woman I had gotten to know fairly well. She told me that earlier that week, one of her white colleagues, with whom she shared identical credentials and seniority, had gotten a promotion. I asked how she responded. She shared, "You know, I don't want to assume anything unfair is going on, so I asked what I could do to get the same promotion."

"What information did you get from management?"

"Well, that's the thing. It's the same story I've heard before, to be honest. They say there isn't an official process for moving up the ladder."

"Hmmm," I said.

"Yeah," she replied. I know we were thinking the same thing. "If there is no process, how does a company expect or presume that promotions make any sense? Inequity and personal bias are totally baked into the non-process."

Make a clear process for career advancements and a transparent set of expectations and criteria for raises and promotions. Extend opportunities that enable BIPOC to gain the experience they need to meet those criteria. Of course, individuals need to be self-driven and take initiative, but they also need to be given the space and support to do that.

DIVERSIFY YOUR CIRCUMSTANCES

In every situation, look around and ask yourself who else should be in the conversation. *Who's there? Who needs to be there? Who's included, and what decision-making power do they have? Who else could benefit from being a part of the discussion and the outcomes?* If you're talking about a group of people, or about a situation that impacts particular people, and none of them are in the room, that's a huge red flag. Like a nonprofit outlining strategies for their services without those they serve in the room or a leadership team setting goals and metrics for an incoming DEI role without that person yet in their seat, it shows you that you're making decisions on behalf of others who are likely capable of contributing to that conversation and decision. At any given time, the people making the decisions should represent the people in the community—whether it's an industry community or a geographic community.

Reach out to conferences, panels, or other business events if only white people are represented in their programming. This has been bugging me quite a bit lately. I'm not sure why it keeps happening. Speaking up when learning opportunities represent only a fraction of the population is one way to demonstrate to organizers that you—and hopefully others—are paying attention. As a white person, if you are asked to participate in an event, you might decline unless they have a diverse roster of people in the lineup. You might suggest one or two BIPOC in your industry who would be a good fit for the topic. I have an acquaintance who was asked to curate a list of interviews from a widely known publisher's podcast collection. Not one Black person had been interviewed, and only one Asian was represented in the list. My acquaintance's response (as an accomplice) was to turn down the request because of the lack of representation and then offer a list of Black professionals who would make excellent interview choices as the publisher moves forward. I have seen high-profile speakers include diversity riders for their engagements. We all might not have the confidence or clout to reject significant opportunities, but there are always chances for you to speak up, even if you're just attending an event.

MODEL INCLUSIVE BEHAVIOR

In the same way that leaders can set trends, you can set practices. Modeling antiracist behavior gives other people the courage to behave in the same way. We know it takes time to learn a new behavior or habit and integrate it into your life and practices. A study found that it takes 66 to 234 days for behaviors to become habits.[60] When you model behaviors and live every day as an antiracist for a while, it becomes a part of who you are. And the more people see you and know that it's possible to live that way, the more likely they are to do it too.

I started this business because people always said to me, "I don't know what to do. I don't know how to start." That is where modeling can be an effective nudge. If more folks have the courage to operate with an accomplice lifestyle, others can see it happening around them and opt in more easily.

If you are in a leadership role or a managerial role, refuse to be silent about your choice to be antiracist—that is how you create the environment you want in your workplace. You can't ask other people to behave in a way that you, yourself, don't. You can't ask people to help create an inclusive work environment where everybody feels welcomed, valued, and supported if you are not living up to that standard. Leaders who model behavior in a workplace give folks the courage to opt in to the work and engage in practices that make space for more folks to be antiracists. Every level and type of action that we encounter on our antiracist journey can be modeled: the successes, the challenges, and the failures.

I admit, there is risk in modeling behavior. You have to be okay with people being angry or upset with you because you chose an antiracist path. And trust me, someone will be upset that you have

---

[60] As found in the study "How are habits formed: Modeling habit formation in the real world" by Phillippa Lally, Cornelia H. M. van Jaarsveld, Henry W. W. Potts, and Jane Wardle in 2009.

chosen to do this work and will ask you to explain yourself. You have to be firm and truly committed.

Modeling behavior also means opting in with a different level of fervor. You're always opting in. You're never missing an opportunity to participate, which means there is a risk of getting tired, and you can't get tired. We need people to stay in the accomplice role, and for a while. That's in part why choosing your lane is so important: we need accomplices who are in it for the long haul, who choose wisely and then set good examples of the work in that space for others. Modeling doesn't mean "do all the things"; it means to do what you can well and show people what it's like.

If modeling behavior sounds a little scary, here is a story about a client who was doing the opposite and how that can be scary too. I was working with a leadership team on antiracism education, and during a session, they revealed that they hadn't told their staff that they had engaged an antiracism coach. I think they were nervous that if people knew, they would be critical of whether the team was doing a good job at it. But truly, not telling people—not openly modeling their learning and doing—did a disservice to the leadership team and the company as a whole. When we hold back or do antiracist work only behind closed doors, we miss a huge opportunity because staff may think, "Well, what are y'all doing anyway?" And if nobody wants to talk about the DEIAA work, then staff may think, "If they're not gonna do any work to be better leaders, then I don't need to do any work to be a better employee." If you're not transparent about what it is you're doing and the why behind what you're doing, you will never be able to achieve outcomes companywide. It takes time to explain to people what you're doing and why you're doing it, and yes, modeling behaviors opens you up to criticism, but it also gets you buy-in along the way.

TRAIN WITH YOUR TEAMS

If you're a leader committed to antiracist work, and you've said it's a priority, you have to ensure training and accountability for everyone on the team—everyone. I believe there is an ideal order for engaging with the work. The entire leadership team should go through training and education first. The experience positions them to speak to the work, to expectations, and set an educated tone in internal conversations about why it's so important to the company. Next, training should happen across all staff. Every department, location, and silo. And leadership should take part in that all-staff training. Going through the work twice can only sharpen their awareness, right?

I know leaders sometimes bristle at going through training with staff. I suspect it goes back to this fear of looking ignorant or messing up in front of your organization. And you might! I can't say you won't, but after years of doing this, I promise that the benefits of everyone engaging together in the same conversations far outweigh the potential mistakes. First, when the leadership is present, it demonstrates that the work is important and communicates that the training is a priority. Second, going through the experience and lessons together creates a shared understanding and language, which is a crucial factor in finding success as a team. Third, every single person must do it because shared accountability and responsibility are the only way to change the culture. One person or one team can't effectively create a sense of company wide inclusion.

APOLOGIZE PROMPTLY AND HONESTLY

We all have to apologize at times. Maybe you think I am an expert at being an accomplice, but this is a lifelong journey for everyone. In a recent group session I hosted on Zoom, I was calling on individuals to share their thoughts about one of our topics. I said, "Juan, do you want to go next?"

There was a heavy pause and a few glances around the Zoom boxes. Then I realized his name was José, not Juan. I felt terrible. I know what it feels like to be BIPOC and being called a name that is clearly associated with your racial identity—it's crappy. You feel like you're reduced to a stereotype in the blink of an eye.

"I got that all the way wrong. I'm sorry."

José assured me, "That's okay, it's fine." And a few others in the group added, "You didn't mean to, it was just a slip of the tongue."

"No, it's not okay." I said, "I don't get to just make that mistake and not address the obvious unconscious bias from which it came."

I honestly felt terrible, but after the session, I realized it was a learning opportunity for others (though I wish it hadn't been at José's expense). Owning your actions and apologizing is not easy, and it's especially not easy in real time. But for a leader, it's possible and it's productive. I received a short message later that day from someone in that cohort: "Seena, I could see how bad you felt about calling José by the wrong name. You did a great job of modeling how to make amends and then pick ourselves up from unintentional damage. It is always impactful for me to see hard things done with such grace, and I definitely learned in that moment." We will all make mistakes as we go, but that's not a reason to disengage: Those are actually some of our strongest opportunities.

DEFINE YOUR SUCCESS BY HOW MUCH YOU RISK TO EMPOWER AND CHAMPION BIPOC

Professional success is usually defined by how far we make it up the ladder, how many sales we close, or the caliber of the companies listed on our resumes. In other words: it's all about us, our journey, our accomplishments. But what if you were to risk that traditional communities. Do you know how your go-to retailers feel about social or political issues? Dig into how they run their companies and ensure that their practices aren't harming people, damaging communities, or making our current social and political situation worse.

For companies, it's twofold. First, it's about spending money with vendors and suppliers who mirror your values. Who are your vendors and clients? Do they have business practices that harm individuals or historically underrepresented groups disproportionately? Are you as vocal as you can be with every person and organization you do business with about your position on race, equity, and inclusion? Second, how can you use your economic clout in your neighborhood, city, or region to lobby for policies and practices that align with your values? If your company does philanthropic work within the community, who is it giving money and resources to? If you work at a foundation that gives money to organizations, do your recipients represent your antiracist values?

Redistributing the wealth that some groups have accumulated at the expense of others is vital. For example, more thriving Black-owned businesses may result in banks being more likely to give out business loans to Black people. More thriving minority-owned businesses may also result in neighborhood revitalization because more and more people would be going to new places to spend money. And if we see more success from companies with leaders from historically underrepresented groups, we will see more diverse leaders.

AND FINALLY, DO THE WORK *AT WORK*

As I've said throughout the book, this is all self-work that starts with who we are. But I also want to emphasize that bringing that self-work to your professional environment is just as important. Taking the risk of bringing your antiracist practice to work will take you farther than quotas or metrics. It's how you actually change the way work feels for individuals.

I started The Woke Coach so that no one would feel like I felt in that job where I was failing. I felt unsupported, excluded, and terribly isolated. So, yes, this is about you being the best, most empathetic human you can be, and then applying everything about that at work. To help connect some dots, I've added a new column to the table from Chapter 1 to help you see a fuller picture of what we've covered in this book.

Accomplices:	Accomplices at Work:
Center race when engaging with issues	Take a race-first perspective when considering policies and decisions
Know they are responsible for changing things	Initiate conversations and ask questions regardless of a person's rank or position
Use their power and privilege for the benefit of others	Share the table, spotlight, and access to projects with people from historically excluded groups
Opt in every day regardless of their own personal circumstances	Define their why and use it to continuously stay active
Integrate antiracism into daily decisions and choices	Have a mindset that is open to race being an important aspect of every experience
Exhibit antiracist behaviors	Do not shy away from engaging others around race, racism, and antiracism
Are partners	Participate in the changes that are necessary because it's everyone's job

Seek to make things equitable	Understand the difference between *equitable* and *equal* and strive to engage with difference
Follow the lead of BIPOC and create communities/cultures of learning with other white folks	Bring others along and provide spaces for white people to learn without burdening BIPOC
Take action on the issues	Do not wait for mandates or quotas to start to make change in their workplace
Disavow the desire or right to be comfortable all the time	Are okay with rocking the boat or calling out systemic issues
Know where they fit in, when to act, and when to listen	Have identified their lane and pursue change in that space
Take risks to address damaging situations	Speak up on behalf of others even when it's difficult because not speaking up causes more damage
Labor on behalf of others	Know that their own success depends on how much they support historically excluded groups
Know *how we got* to the place we're at with racial inequity	Deepen their analysis around every issue to explore any possible racial or racialized implications
Empathize with the people who are affected by racial inequity	Believe that lived experiences are different for different racialized people and know their place within that reality

Are self-sufficient in antiracist behaviors, actions, and learning (proactive)	Create learning circles and accountability circles to ensure they are continuously learning
Believe we have a moral imperative to take action when circumstances are not equitable	Seek out opportunities to make organizations and teams more equitable
Can identify and move past their defensiveness or overwhelm to take action	Know it's not about them, it's about the systems
Know to pause, consider, and then react	Can set aside personal feelings to act on behalf of the greater good

CHAPTER 11: YOUR PATH FORWARD

Are You Going to Do the Work?

Recently, a colleague and I unpacked our work with a particular client and compared what we had observed over the time as their leaders learned to practice accompliceship. The before description included *fractured*, *tired*, *frustrated*, and *self-sabotaging*. The after description was much richer. The client was excited about their ability to speak to race and issues around race and beyond. They were excited to be engaged in a company that valued them personally and their ability to create inclusive circumstances for others. They got to see potential versions of themselves beyond just who they were in that moment. They were released from whatever ideas and assumptions they'd had of themselves and their colleagues before and felt more confident in who they could become. As leaders, they were feeling safe and brave. In our vulnerable conversations about race and equity, their feelings and fears were being acknowledged. They realized, through the course of our time together, that they didn't actually know each other that well, and the conversations we asked them to have around identity and experience helped them deepen their relationships. Ultimately, they escaped the isolation that can happen when we don't fully engage with people openly and wholly and felt closer to each other and their own true selves.

From clients, I hear that once they deployed the Three A's and purposefully engaged in an antiracist practice, they had tremendous outcomes. They:

- Improved their recruitment and hiring practices
- Got more intentional about making time and space for the work that DEIAA requires
- Introduced more effective affinity and employee resource group spaces
- Developed strategic inclusion plans with metrics and measurable outcomes
- Created equity frameworks to ensure they were asking the right questions
- Had better conversations with all employees, and the lines of communication opened wider

One of the leaders we worked with wrote us this note about what's possible when you do this work: "Going into this, I knew that I've had the benefit of white privilege. I also knew that there was systemic racism indoctrinated into our culture. What I did not know was the lengths it stretched. Learning about voter suppression, gerrymandering, fair housing, incarceration, slavery, and the list goes on, has opened my eyes to the fact that the playing field is not even, and while there has been significant improvement from generation to generation, our problems are far from solved. . . . While I'm angry and disheartened, I'm also hopeful and optimistic. . . . I find hope in myself, knowing that while all these problems feel so big, it only takes one to make a change."

This could be you.

You are not here only to listen, witness, or observe. That is the beginning, but there is more. Inclusion will take work because this has never been done before. We talk about leadership and leadership qualities and say, "Leaders need to be strong. They need to be self-assured. They need to be visionary. They need to be like a shepherd, have a high IQ, and be an empath." We have molded our idealized style of leadership with precise and high expectations, but nobody ever says leaders need to be antiracists. Until now. I'm not saying those other things aren't important, but being an antiracist is super important. And if at some point in business school, a professor or visiting CEO said, "You should probably use an race-first lens to be an empath or develop an antiracist practice to have more emotional intelligence," we wouldn't be having this conversation because leaders would have done their damnedest to do achieve all of those set expectations.

There is urgency to what we're doing here—to righting our historic wrongs. And there is urgency in becoming the best, most understanding, empathetic version of yourself around issues of antiracism, bias, equity, and injustice. Building our capabilities to create equity is how we will engage with all of humanity. If you don't develop your ability to create inclusion, how will you lead people to build new things for our changing world or lead people to find connections and relationships at work?

Workplaces don't have to be toxic; that's not what work is supposed to be. I think, over time, we've come to expect that workplaces will always have some toxic elements—those are the dues we pay. But this isn't necessary or normal. It's an excuse not to do better. We know that's not effective; enough research has been done that no leader can ignore the fact that toxic environments are not conducive to good work. Collectively, we know enough now to do things differently. And now that you know how to practice accompliceship, *you* know enough to do things differently and produce different outcomes and experiences for the people around you.

With all of this work, we're creating honest, real relationships. That's it. We're trying to tap into humanity and connect with other people. It sounds so simple, but the key to achieving it is equity. The reality is that our current inequitable situation is harming everyone. Period. It's keeping white people from understanding the people around them, rendering them deficient to such a degree that they cannot lead diverse teams. It is keeping BIPOC from participating to their full capacity in our workplaces and in our industries. These inequities keep all of us from knowing each other in honest ways. If someone doesn't believe me about the racism I've experienced, then there is no way for me to trust them about anything else. And our country will break because of this.

As leaders, we can't just rest on who we are. We have to continually think about who we want to be. Who we are today isn't enough, and the environments in which we have succeeded are not enough for *everyone* to thrive.

Once you have relationships, everything else will be easier because you will have a foundation upon which to build. Whether you're a leader of teams or an individual out in the world, once you know a person—the whole of them—you have the trust to more fully engage and offer support. If, as a leader, you're simply trying to answer a specific question or solve a company problem, you're missing the real opportunity in this work. When you go deeper and develop real connections, you get to be more of your full, honest self, and others do too. In that environment, you can get to the real root causes of everything.

THIS IS A CONTINUOUS, LIFELONG JOURNEY

I really want you—and everyone—to speak truth to circumstance when you witness injustice. That means naming what we can all see but no one is saying out loud. I had a client who hired a Muslim man but didn't provide a prayer room. An accomplice would speak truth to that circumstance: "He needs a prayer room. We make all kinds of accommodations for people, like allowing smoke breaks, but we're not providing our colleague with something that is part and parcel of who he is and what he needs." Or perhaps a truth to name is that you're in a company doing DEIAA work, and the leadership team is entirely white. Being confident and educated enough to name things takes deeply personal, introspective work coupled with education. We all have to unlearn the biased historical narratives and lessons we took in as children and young adults. And we now have the opportunity to relearn everything we "know" about history, systems, traditions, cultures, and institutions with a new lens—the lens of an accomplice.

You already have what you need to make a difference. When we broadly talk about making a difference, we're not talking about each person, like you, singlehandedly overhauling everything racist. It's defeating to think about inequity as one huge issue. We have to ask, "What are the specific steps I can take in my life to create the world I want to live in?" And then we have to take those steps. We each have a sphere of influence in our personal and professional lives and in our communities, and we each have interests and talents we can put to good use. How can you lend your talents to a cause? How can you share your antiracist journey and your reasons for starting the journey with people in your life? This is how we change our collective circumstances: all of us taking intentional steps to increase equity.

I struggled with how much specific direction and advice I could give you in this book. Maybe you want to know exactly what to do to become an accomplice and apply a racial equity lens and ultimately do all that at work. But even if I could do that, it wouldn't serve you in the way you think it might. It's never about having all the answers or knowing the exact thing to do at every moment. It's about awareness, analysis, and action.

This is a lifelong and very personal journey on which you will always be learning more. I cannot itemize every single to-do for every single person. The perspective I give you here in this book is a springboard, a way to orient your ongoing awareness, analysis, and action. That part of the journey is yours to take and yours to make.

There will always be a new challenge, but if you have a strong practice and the right mental tools, you will be able to figure it out if you:

Remember:

- Race, a made-up construct, and racism, the power hierarchy assigned to race, are our oldest and most persistent problems and still impact us today.
- White supremacy culture has permeated our culture and must be dismantled for *all* people to thrive.
- Privilege is the unearned access you possess; power is the action you take using your privilege.

Then ask:

- How might race be playing into this situation?
- How is *my* race shaping my interactions?
- How can I continuously opt into antiracist action?
- What information or perspectives am I missing?
- How am I widening my aperture?
- Now that I know more, what will I do?

Remember the Three A's:

- Awareness: What do I know now that I didn't know before?
- Analysis: What do I need to learn?
- Action: How do I do something with this information?

We always have been and always will be in this together. We are all part of the human race together, even when there is division, tension, and violence. Making our collective reality better is shared responsibility. It is on you, and me, and everyone around us. Join me, join others. We are here for you.

Let's do this.

Get woke, stay woke, be woke: Hire The Woke Coach. Sign-up for our mailing list. Join our community of fierce, engaged accomplices at www.thewokecoach.com.

ACKNOWLEDGEMENTS

I would like to express my deepest gratitude to the following people.

Ansa Akyea — For all things at all times in all ways.

Cashton and Senam — Learning from and through you has always been the best gift.

The Woke Coach Team— Oforiwa Akyea, Shameika Black, Ilene Governale, Angela Harder, Catrina Huynh, Aleena Kaleem, Sonja McCall, Traci Norum, Toni Oberto, Shradha Parekh, Nora Patterson, Sara Richardson, and Liz Schumacher

Dara Beevas and the team at Wise Ink, Lyz Nagan, Nora McInerny, Joshua Dorothy, Michael Robertson, Ty Defoe, Tracy Nielsen, Alex West Steinman, John Christakos, Maurice Blanks, Amy Langer, David Wilson, Dave Murphy, Ellen Wilson, Amanda Brinkman, Nadege Souvenir, Ashley Aram, Tema Okun, Kenneth Jones, and every The Woke Coach client since 2018!